Italian American Soul

An Anthology

Tales of Italian culture, behavior,
traditions, customs, and aspects
of life as experienced by
Italian Americans

Edward Albert Maruggi

Copyright © 2004 by Winston Publishing
                52 Tobey Court
                Pittsford, New York 14534-1857
                Fax: 585-385-7953
                www.winstonpublishing.us
                email: winston@winstonpublishing.us

This book was set in Palatino and Comic Sands MS fonts on Aldus Pagemaker Version 7.0 and Photoshop 5.5 using an iMac computer, a Lexmark Z73 Printer/Color Copier/ Scanner and a UMAX Astra 1220U Scanner.

First Edition

Printed in the United States of America

Library of Congress Control Number: 2003098863

ISBN 0-9658870-1-4

Cover Designer: Antonio Toscano

Printed by: Victor Graphics
                1121 Bernard Drive
                Baltimore, MD 21223

∞ Dedication ∞

To my parents Teresa Molino Maruggi and Antonio Maruggi who emigrated from southern Italy in 1905 and 1907, respectively, and who lived all of the emotions, culture, traditions, customs, and behaviors described herein.

∞ Acknowledgements ∞

It would be extremely difficult to provide individual kudos to the many contributors to this project. Italian Americans from across the country submitted tales in prose and poetry related to the suggested topical areas involving the Italian American experience. Of the six hundred and twenty-five letters mailed to Italian Americans as well as a few sent to those who have been or are intimately knowledgeable of the Italian American life style, one hundred and fifteen persons submitted stories. Of that number, ninety-nine tales were selected to become part of this anthology. I regret that all submissions could not be accepted. I received tales via e-mail, fax, hard copy, CD, audio tapes, and through individual taped interviews.

I obtained the names of possibile contributors from friends, associates, peers, colleagues, and family mailing lists. I contributed stories, compiled the accepted tales, typed them, and provided a cursory edit of the book, The editor, however, was Harriet Solit, a woman who deserves most of the credit for the quality of the book. Her professional approach to editing and proofreading of the book was outstanding She is an artist who loves Italy, the Italian people, and its culture. She is a versatile person with varied interests, for whom I have great respect.

Forty percent of the tales were submitted by Italian Americans living in the Rochester/Monroe County area of New York State. Most of the remaining contributions came from the northeastern states, but others were also received from Florida, Iowa, Texas, California as well as from other midwest communities. Several contributors provided photos of special people or events related to their submissions. The front page of each topic contains a photo related to one of the tales on that topic.

Many of the contributors are current members of the Italian American Historical Society (AIHA) of which I am a member. This organization provided the impetus for this project having peaked my interest in "things Italian." For that I am truly grateful.

Very special thanks, however, go to my wife, Carolyn, who continues to support me in the various endeavors in which I have become involved. She has offered invaluable assistance to this project. Contributions by my children; son Edward P., daughter Susan Maruggi Stokes and niece Virginia Mesolella Graf were pleasant surprises. Close friends who have stories in the book include Vincent Fazio, Eddie and Fran Gala, Joe Boccaccino, Charlie and Terry Marino, Vincent Natale, Nick Morante, and Joe Mileo. For their input, many thanks.

My very good friend, Antonio Toscano, designed the cover for the book. He is a professor at Rochester Institute of Technology and a fellow wine maker. His expertise in the field of imaging and computer graphics is very much appreciated.

*We must accept all the implications of
our human experience, one of the most
important of which is the small scope
of biologically transmitted behavior,
and the enormous role of the cultural
process in the transmission of tradition.*

*What really binds men together is their
cultures, their ideas, and the standards
they have in common.*

Ruth Benedict
Patterns of Cultures (1934)

MONTERIGGIONE

HARRIET SOLIT

∞ Contents ∞

∞ Introduction ∞

My mother came to America with her family in the spring of 1905. Family members on the journey included her mother and father and five of their other children. It was her father's third trip to America, this time to bring his family to New York City, where two other children were born. Three years in New York City provided few employment opportunities for her father so in 1908 the family moved to the west side of Rochester, New York where an enclave of immigrant Italians was beginning to form.

My father emigrated in 1907 from the same village as Ma. They were both born in Melfi, in Basilicata in Italy's poor south. At age seventeen Pa came here with several other friends from Melfi, but with none of his family. He left his mother, father and sister behind. He never returned to Italy and never saw them again.

My parents married in 1910 in Rochester, New York where Ma gave birth to four children. I am the youngest of those children. Before all of the children married we lived in the Italian American section of the "Dutchtown" area of Rochester's west side.

My Italian ancestry and subsequent life experiences while living in an Italian American neighborhood have had a tremendous impact on who I am and how I behave as an individual. Ma and Pa had a great deal to do with that.

Authoring and publishing a book entitled, "Mushrooms, Sausage, and Wine: Life With An Immigrant Father," allowed me to look back at the various experiences that my parents and my environment provided during my formative years and into my early married life. At the time, most of these experiences and events seemed so trivial or nondescript, but the human brain has a way of tucking these experiences away for future reference.

Having reflected upon those Italian American cultural experiences involving family, relatives, and friends while growing up, I thought that I might wish to share mine with others with the same heritage, and that others might want to do the same. Hence the origin of this project.

Edward Albert Maruggi

Family and Friends

Lucia Means Light

∞ A Job For Papa ∞

It was in the summer of 1938, when Papa walked slowly up to our fourth floor apartment on Fulton Avenue in the Bronx his head drooping with shame; he had been laid off from his job at the Herrmann Lumber Yard where he had been employed for twenty years. For the first time in his life Papa was without work, without hope, and worst of all, without the pride that had been his main strength as head of our family. How would the rent of thirty-seven dollars a month get paid? A family of six could not live on my sister's salary of eighteen dollars a week. How would Papa, who had been brought to the lumberyard by one of his Umbrian *Paesani* when he first immigrated, even know how to look for a job without feeling the he was seeking charity?

Upon being refused employment at several lumberyards in the area, one evening Papa pushed his dinner plate aside.

"What's wrong?" my mother asked with a concerned look on her face.

"I'm not working, so I don't deserve to eat."

My brother Gino announced that he would leave college to look for work to help support the family. This further wounded Papa's pride. Without a word he rose from the table and retreated to his bedroom.

Later, as I lay awake in my bed I vowed that whoever was responsible for bringing such misery to my family would not sleep so well, either.

The following morning, I put on my peach and blue flowered voile dress with puffed sleeves and tight-fitting blue taffeta bodice that Mama had made for me for my fifteenth birthday, almost a year ago, and for which I had received many, many compliments.

When I headed toward the door I held in my hand a brown paper bag with a half-finished red wool sweater I was knitting. I told Mama that I needed help with it and I was going next door to have my friend help me. In my other hand I clutched two nickels for carfare.

With quiet determination I boarded the 3rd Avenue El and rode it to 138th Street, descended the long stairway to the sidewalk, and walked towards the river to the Herrmann Lumber Company. I hesitantly walked past drunks at the curb, and derelicts who voiced indecent remarks in my direction. There was not another child or woman in sight. My insides were trembling but I could not afford to turn back and lose my carfare.

Upon seeing me, the surprised receptionist at the lumberyard office slid back the frosted window and asked,

"What is it you want?"

"I'd like to speak to the owner of the company, please."

"And whom should I say you are?"

"Miss Medori."

"And what do you wish to see him about?"

"It's personal."

She ushered me into a large paneled room with two huge oak desks with a young man sitting behind each of them –one dark-haired, one blond – nephews of the original owners. They asked me to sit in one of two chairs in the room and waited for me to speak.

In a torrent of tears, I blurted out all the thoughts that had been swimming around in my brain for two weeks; how my father had worked so hard for the company for twenty years; how cruel they had been to let him go now that he was an old man of forty-six and couldn't possibly find a job somewhere else. He was so despondent; and how my brother was planning to leave college; and how I wouldn't be able to have a sweet- sixteen party.

"I didn't know Adolfo had a family," one nephew turned and said to the other.

"How many children in the family," he asked me.

"Four, sir."

The two man exchanged quizzical looks. The blond nodded as though he had read the other's mind.

" Well, young lady, there must have been some mistake. We didn't let your father go. He still has a job with us," he said politely.

My elation was suddenly interrupted by fear, fear of what my father might do to me for having gone over his head.

"My father must never know of my coming here today," I stated pleadingly. I picked up the bag with the knitting,

"I'm suppose to be at a friends house ———.″

I hardly noticed the derelicts on the way home or the homeless people at the curb. I had done it. I had not wasted the ten cents carfare. I was so delirious with joy that I forgot the knitting bag on the subway car.

After I arrived at home, I casually asked my mother into my bedroom and confided to her what I had done. She promised not to tell my father, and kissing me said, "You did the right thing." She did not keep her promise, however. Sometime later, I overheard my parents whispering in the kitchen but, to my amazement, I also heard, for the first time in two weeks, Papa laughing —— a low quiet laugh of relief. The next day Papa received a telegram asking him to return to work at the Herrmann Lumber Company where he was gainfully employed for an additional twenty years. I typed a proper letter of thanks to the two men who listened to me; Papa never mentioned the matter to me.

Two years later, one of the bosses approached Papa, wanting to know if I had graduated from high school yet because they wanted to offer me a job in their office. Papa told them that I had graduated long ago, at the age of sixteen, and held a responsible position with a prominent steamship company.

Viola Medori Labozzetta

∞ An Act of Respect ∞

My father, who was born in Italy, came to America when he was six years old and, therefore, being fluent in English spoke it with no accent. My mother came at the age of twenty, learned English on her own, and spoke with a heavy Italian accent like some of her siblings and in-laws. When my parents were speaking to me as well as to my brothers and sisters, they spoke English. When they were in the presence of my aunts and uncles, they used Italian out of consideration for those who, while to some degree or another were bilingual, felt it easier to speak their first language, Italian. Very often in this language, that I did not understand, I would hear them address one another as *Mister Joe* or *Donna Frances*. Somehow I knew that they were addressing one another with a little more respect than the use of only the first name would allow.

If my aunts and uncles or other relatives wanted to be casual, they used only the first name speaking in Italian or in English. If they wanted to add a little respect in English, they would have to use the last name. However, to call someone Mr. Ortolani or Mrs. Montalto would be formal in Italian for such a close friend of relative. Yet, they wanted to bestow upon certain people a light sign of informal respect, so they added the courtesy title *Mister* and *Donna* to the familiar first name. I have found myself still doing this today at different times with family, friends, and colleagues. Too often I receive the response, "Oh, why the formality?" Somehow I feel something is missing in our English language customs today that existed in my parent's life.

Vincent Ortolani

∞ Italian Homestead Offers Second Chance ∞

My family has a green heart. Not one of envy, but of lush rolling hills where medieval cities crown mountaintops and offer themselves up to the heavens. My grandfather forsook this Umbrian land for oppressive East Harlem in New York City and can only be understood within its context: he was an adventurous man in hard times, a man determined always to better himself and his family, a risk taker as we would call him today. He left behind his brother to care for his widowed mother. My grandfather married a Southerner, a Calabrian woman who had also recently arrived in America. He labored in a lumberyard in Manhattan; she took in homework, embroidering tablecloths, and later worked in factories that produced women's apparel.

Early in their married life, they managed to take their children up to a boarding house on a dairy farm in Westchester County during the summer. They acquired high land adjacent to the dairy farm where tall pines met green fields at the perimeter. Eventually, they created a paradise for their children's children. I was born into this paradise.

Within days, in June, when the school year had finished, we would leave Brooklyn and head upstate. When we turned off route 202 and onto the stony street, passed the turkey farm and the Jesuit Seminary, the anxiety mounted until the car came to a halt. My father shifted the car into low gear and took a left up the hilly, rocky road where high weeds ran down its center and brushed the engine of our vehicle that pulled itself up to the farm's driveway. There, life was surreal. Grape arbors became school buses and upside down benches, boats. Tomatoes from grandpa's garden were known to swell to two pounds and apple - green colored squash grew as long as baseball bats. We threaded pink and white fuschia phlox onto weeds with which to adorn our hair. We learned the art of recycling long before it was a household word: coffee grounds fertilized flower beds, corn husks fed the pigs, wilted lettuce secured from the trash bins behind the A & P nourished the rabbits. Vegetable seeds were dried and planted the following spring, garbage was composted and occasionally burned, tin cans flattened, and containers reused. Oregano was hung in the attic to dry: basil grew in abundance and flavorful homegrown tomatoes were canned for sauce. Chickens and ducks filled the air with their clucking and young deer were bottle-fed oatmeal until they were old and strong enough to be set free.

On Sundays, we returned from church to the welcoming roasts that my grandmother prepared on her wood-fired outdoor oven while she fried zucchini in sizzling olive oil and boiled macaroni on it's stove top.

"Just like in Italy," she would announce. Long tables were set for family members as well as for any guests that might drop by. Grandpa's homemade wine was brought up from the cellar and consumed throughout the week. Evenings found our parents drinking high balls and singing Italian songs, telling jokes and playing cards.

Along with adolescence came the awareness of mortality, and I dreaded the day when my grandparents would cease to be. Would their death cause the world that meant so much to us children to become undone? When I ventured to Italy as a young adult, however, I learned for the first time what this humble estate had signified for my grandparents – my grandfather in particular. On the edge of a rocky dirt road outside the village of Portaria, I found the other half of my family waiting for me. My grandfather's brother, bearing a remarkable likeness to my grandfather, walked me around the property, pointing out olive and chestnut trees that had been replaced by apple, peach, and cherry trees in Westchester. The setup had an uncanny resemblance to the farm, and as I stood in the midst of *this country,* it all became quite clear to me: my grandfather had worked all his life to regain what he had left behind.

My grandparents are long gone and so is the farm which their family found to be unmanageable. America's prosperity has a way of dispersing families: each heir owned his own home and was not only independent of the farm, but encumbered by it. We grandchildren were not yet in a position to purchase the land and keep it in the family.

While loving grandparents, who tried to hold fast to ethnic customs, have nurtured my children, they missed the experience recounted to them through stories, photos, and slides. That is, until I brought them back to the stone house where my grandfather was born and to the land where a late-to-bloom economy had slowed time down. Intergenerational families still lived together: homes were passed down and not readily discarded: family members came together for Sunday meals taken on long cloth covered tables overflowing with food and wine and fruit. And, although contemporaries of my parents, my aunt and uncle took on the persona of my grandparents.

Instead of school in a grape arbor, my children played with their cousins on Roman ruins. They cut slivers of prosciutto from hams hanging in the curing shed.

"It's the closest thing I can imagine to being at the farm," my daughter remarked. And so it has been for me to this day. My grandparents had given me Italy in the farm, and now Italy had given me back my grandparents.

I return often to my Italian homestead. My children, young adults, go off on their own. We last visited as a family in April of last year to celebrate the fiftieth wedding anniversary of my aunt and uncle. As we made the turn off the main road onto a smaller road, my heart began to race. My husband shifted the car into low gear and we made our way along the rocky dirt road where high weeds ran down its center and brushed the engine of the car. The various aromas emanating from the outdoor oven (a modern gas one had replaced the wood-fired one), mixed with odors from the animal pens, and filled my senses. The table was set for thirty. We were home. But the visit was bittersweet this time as mortality nagged again.

"I will not see many more days like these,"my eighty-year-old uncle wishfully confided to me on the day of our departure. Nor I, I thought. There is only one "second chance."

Marisa Labozzetta

∞ **Home** ∞

Heard three people speaking Italian
in the supermarket today
a man, his wife chatting
with a younger woman
in so casual a way.
I parked my cart near them
pretended to study canned vegetables.

But I was listening
recalling the familiar rhythms of the words
watching hand gestures, facial shifts.

The rise and fall of the vowels
remembered sounds of something lost.
Home is the sound of people speaking.

Italian rooted in the kitchen and
curling, like a vine, up the stairs
to my bedroom when I'm falling asleep.
Mama, Papa, Zia Nina, Zio Peppino,
Joe, Elena, Paulo, and Pete
drinking coffee, iced-tea, anisette
eating Sara Lee pound cake and homemade pizzelles.
Cigar smoke and laughter looping toward
the kitchen light in gauzy ribbons.
Cards shuffled, nuts cracked open.

Those laughing grown-up voices
that said to me
no matter who has died or
what has happened or
where we are going

the family will survive.

Marianna, you will do more than survive.
You will rise above your destiny
soar beyond your fortune
will grab fate by the hair
hold it down, kick it
until it agrees to
smile on you with blessings.

Mary Ann Mannino

∞ On Being Resourceful ∞

Pa was a thrifty person in several different ways, never spending money foolishly and always interested in conserving natural resources. He often looked for a bargain or a sale for goods and services. I am certain that this trait was as a result of his family's poor economic situation during his youth in Italy.

For example, when Pa made Italian sausage, he and I trotted down to Front Street, off Main in Rochester, New York, to buy the least expensive pork butts and a few feet of pig intestines for stuffing the prepared sausage meat. Pa also believed it was his responsibility to make sure that we had enough natural gas for cooking, especially around the holidays, so Ma could bake bread, panetone, cannolis, crespelles, calconcelles, and various other pastries for family and friends.

Pa knew that doing all this baking and cooking required the use of a lot of natural gas. As a result, he discovered a method for obtaining free natural gas so as to minimize one of the family's utility bills. This process included turning off the main gas line into the house with a pipe wrench, and with the same wrench he'd disconnect the coupling which connects the line to the gas meter, and insert, of all things, a stay from one of Ma's old corsets. At this point, he reconnected the coupling to the gas line. In some way this procedure allowed for an unlimited use of natural gas to flow at no cost to the consumer because it did not allow the meter to register the amount of fuel flow. After the holiday period ended he carefully reassembled the gas meter and its components so that there would be no recognizable problem when the utility company man came to our house to read the meter.

In summer, Pa needed a lot of water to keep his very large vegetable garden green and lush. During a dry spell when Pa felt the need to water his plants, he'd head down to the basement where the water meter was located and remove the glass cover from the meter's gauge as well as the dial face mechanism. This mechanism recorded the amount of water used. By doing this, Pa was able to water his garden without being charged for the amount of water he used. After each watering, he carefully replaced the meter mechanism so no one could detect what he had done.

For each of these clandestine operations, I was the one who assisted by handing him the tools while he disassembled and then reassembled the components. I guess that made me an accessory to the crimes.

Edward Albert Maruggi

∞ **The Saint** ∞

I remember her waxen face
her shriveled shoulders
the dry lips that baked my cheek
and never formed into a smile

At family dinners
she stayed in the back of the kitchen
while her daughters
served the guests their food

Her brother-in-law nicknamed her the Saint
when she took him in and paid
his cab fare from Ellis Island

In the halcyon days
of her husband's career
she would rise all hours of the night
to feed his cronies

Rumors flew
that her husband's business trips
to Newport, Rhode Island
were really romantic assegnations

She had three sons
but two died young
and she doted on
the sole survivor

The day the Army ordered
him to leave for California
she fell out of her bedroom window

to the pavement two floors below

Her children said
it was an accident
but somehow she ended up
in a psychiatric ward

I remember her 50th
wedding anniversary
how hard
she pulled down
on the arm
of her drunken husband
 as he stood
and extolled her dedication

                                          Gil Fagiani

∞ Lucia Means Light ∞

I grew up among my many family relations at #2222 West Eleventh Street in Brooklyn, a wild and wonderful place that was more a village than just a home and that included relatives living upstairs, downstairs and next door. Grandpa Marco and Grandma Lucia Antonini's household was my family's first residence. A big duplex located on a street with tall oak trees, it had a magical backyard that contained a grape arbor, a modest sized garden in which Grandpa planted tomatoes, zucchini, aromatic Italian herbs and spices which I loved to eat. There was also a fig tree laden with the most delicious fat, juicy figs, when ripe. I would frequently steal several of them to share with neighborhood friends.

Our garage was a type of multipurpose room that sometimes housed an auto, two bicycles, toys, tables and chairs for family fetes and a punching bag. It was placed so high off the floor that I used a tall ladder to reach it for an occasional swing, unless my father was home to boost me up while I punched. We had a wine press and a workroom in the finished basement that Grandpa had built. His work room was filled with curious tools, various size chisels, and vises that I believed came from some kind of medieval torture chamber, an idea that my grandfather did not discourage. Grandpa had these tools because he was a highly creative artisan and sculptor who made expensive furniture for the wealthy during the depression.

I loved watching him create at home on Saturdays. Although he liked to work alone, he did allow me, on occasion, to stand nearby if I remained quiet. I witnessed his fiery passion move into his hands as he repeatedly pounded a solid block of wood for hours with variously shaped hammers and cutting tools until it was transformed into a recognizable form. The block of cedar or pine smelled so delicious when sanded and refined. I felt fortunate when he allowed me to pick up the wood chips from the floor. He created a stool for me that I cherished, a bank he often filled with dollars and coins, and other pieces for our home as well as for his customers. After having suffered a stroke, I watched him teach himself to draw and sculpt all over again with his other hand. Although he recovered only part of his lost skills, our family still retains an accurate likeness of Abraham Lincoln that he patiently and skillfully carved from a piece of mahogany.

Grandma's face turned pink like a cherub's when she danced the tarantella at our house and lightened the conversation when Grandpa was talking politics. Conversations would turn into debates and debates into arguments, until grandma transformed the atmosphere without anyone noticing, except perhaps us children. We all loved her dearly, all four feet eleven inches of her, and I considered her my major ally. Sometimes #2222 would feel like a war zone, especially when grandpa turned our warm kitchen into a furnace during a debate. I enjoyed both the convivial and intense atmospheres.

"Anyone making more than $500,000 a year is a criminal stealing from the people who work for him!" Grandpa blurted in his broken English to our guest and neighbor, Eugene Rubino.

I noticed Mr. Rubino's discomfort and hesitation to challenge grandpa, but I was most pleased that the attention had shifted away from me. If I was lucky, the adults might not discover that I hadn't eaten my supper.

"The rich I've worked for were selfish and prejudiced. They'd use me and they'd make you sweat to collect. I carved the beds they slept in, but they'd send me around to the back door to enter the house. They believe every Italian is a Fascist or a member of the Mafia, and that's their excuse for not paying up," grandpa expounded.

"Marco, don't you think you're too hard on the rich? You can't blame all our problems on rich people. Besides, what makes you think that wealth gives people imagination? They don't understand what our lives are like," Mr. Rubino replied, defensively.

"Why are you defending them Eugene?" He thundered.

"I'm not. I'm just pointing out that there are good and bad people among the rich and the poor," Marco retorted. "The rich are worse because they have the means to help people. They saw the bread lines, the poor selling apples for a dime and heartlessly walked away in their fine minks and diamonds, blind to the suffering. You are a working man and a taxpayer. You saw what went on during the depression. The people I worked for on the hill tried to beat me out of every penny I earned and never cared to ask how many mouths I had to feed. Greed is ugly and more insatiable than hunger. Greed destroyed Italy and if the *Medagones* (Americans) aren't careful, it'll destroy them too."

"I have to challenge you there, Marco. You can't assume that all rich people are greedy. I know many a poor man who is more greedy and criminal, too."

" Tell me how many rich people you know. They remain far removed from our class," grandpa snapped.

With forefinger pointed at grandpa, Mr. Rubino angrily stated,

"If you're not careful, Antonini, people will brand you a Communist! Remember what happened to Michael Grimaldi."

A hush fell over the room, because everyone, even I, knew about Michael Grimaldi.   He was raised by his resourceful grandmother Rose and grandfather Pasquale who received a meager monthly disability check as a result of a work related accident. They raised Michael because he lost his parents and three siblings to tuberculosis. Despite devastating hardships Michael attended City College of New York on a full scholarship. While there he became involved with a socialist group and was expelled and hounded for years until he left the city, marrying a woman radical, who they called Hebrew (for Jewish).

Eugene's remark made grandpa's blood boil.

"I'm not afraid of name calling, nor am I afraid of McCarthy and his terrorists. If the Black Hand couldn't intimidate me when I had my own business, why should I fear a group of ignorant and ambitious politicians? People love to dismiss the truth with a label. Besides, there are no real Communists. Stalin was a Fascist!" That's when grandma stepped in.

"Have another glass of wine Eugene. You know Marco and the boys made it themselves," she purposefully stated as she climbed up on a small stool her husband had made to help her compensate for her lack of height. Stretching for a serving dish high over head she exclaimed with gusto,

"Oh to be tall like one of those Swedes. What lucky people. Why did God make me so short? In my next life, I want to be at least six feet tall."

By now everyone was laughing. They knew grandma wanted two things in this life, a college education and height.

"You must eat more of your dinner, Lucia. There are people in China who are starving" grandpa said with true conviction.

"She's eaten enough. Don't force her," grandma chimed. Her droll face and bright blue-gray eyes cheered me while I stood up to one of my worst culinary enemies, split pea soup, second only to *coccozze* (zucchini). I am sure I was allergic to both, certainly too young to digest them. Why wouldn't the adults listen to me? Rolling my eyes back into their sockets, I tried to down another spoonful of the gritty textured stuff, but gagged. I could see grandfather weakening, but then mother stepped in.

"Enough of the melodrama, young lady! You haven't been eating all week. You can't live on meatballs and macaroni alone. Finish that soup or there will be no TV for you tonight," she remarked mercilessly.

I tried to control my reactions. Medicine would have been easier. I didn't want to miss TV. Bed could feel like a prison of such loss and grief when I was missing an activity that grown ups were engaged in. Tonight we were going to watch the opera "Pagliacci" and I would get to see grandpa cry. If the hour were later, my father would be home from work and save me.

The doorbell sounded a possible reprieve. Could this be my father? The door opened to the tall dark man with soft blue eyes like a film star of the nineteen forties. Sweeping me up for a kiss and a hug, our usual greeting, father also kissed mother and grandma before sitting opposite grandpa at the other end of the table. What powerful and comforting arms father has. Surely he'll spare me.

"You're home early for a change," mother said, pleased that he was home from the factory before seven.

"We had a good day; all the garments were on time," he replied. Looking directly at me he asked,

"And how was your day today, young lady? Did you enjoy school? Were you well behaved?"

Dinner was the hour of reckoning. I wanted to be sure I could claim a near perfect day before being excused from finishing my supper.

"Don't even think of buttering up your father so you can skip the pea soup. There are enough vegetables in it to make a complete meal." Oh, No! I thought, mother had seen right through my naive, six year-old mind. Now father may not do what I had hoped for. I knew that he would not risk quarreling. With a deep sigh he said,

"Split green soup, again."

He wasn't pleased either. Maybe I still have a chance.

"But let's eat up anyway, Lulu. You heard what your mother said about the vegetables." Mother jumped in with,

"If you don't stop these antics, you will be sent to bed with the baby."

Tonight, mother was in charge. Some nights it was father. I decided to back off. Grandma finally brought a conclusion to my dilemma by silently lifting my plate and clearing out the remaining soup without anyone noticing. Darkness was a time for family sharing in a space called the family room, the hub of each evening's activities after supper. Here, there was a feeling of closeness, warmth and security. This room housed the TV as well as many exotic furnishings made and collected by grandpa.

I grew up with the sound of opera all around me.

Grandpa loved opera and we often enjoyed listening to it on radio, the Victrola, as well as on TV. I always listened attentively because he had promised to take me to the Metropolitan Opera house when I was old enough to appreciate them. I never really understood operas, except that the stories were often filled with tragic events, overflowing with jealousy, passion, and death.

Voices of the divas and tenors moved me so, and despite a language barrier, the language of feelings in the operas reached ranges that were infinitely exciting and enticing. On this night the narrator had explained enough of the plot in between each of the acts to keep me interested.

Grandma loved the music, costumes, and pageantry, but thought that the central character's behavior was silly.

"Why doesn't he just start over again and forget his wife?" She questioned. "I lost my first husband, nobody wants to lose someone, but sometimes we do, that's no reason to murder another human being."

"Rispetto, Mama, rispetto," grandpa said vehemently with an assurance that implied we'd be daft not to see it his way.

"How could a man live with any self respect if his wife cuckolds him," he asked forming the sign of horns by extending the forefinger and little finger of his right hand. Grandma just shrugged.

"That's right!" My father said.

"Maybe not to kill, but, his honor must be defended; infidelity is a disgrace. Marriage is for life," he concluded in a funereal tone.

" That's old fashioned and ridiculous," mother replied. "That woman had no life. While he was off being a star on stage, she was left home alone. It's no wonder she left him for another man," she said while staring into my father's eyes.

I found myself in agreement with my mother. With all

the courage and authority I could muster, I piped, "I think the old clown is full of pride. He didn't kill his wife because he loved her. He killed her because he couldn't bear to see her happy without him."

And all the grown-ups listened!!

Louisa Calio

∞ Angela's Fruit ∞

My paternal grandmother, Angela Puccia, who lived in the farmlands of the mountaintop village of Pulcherini, kept her own last name all her life. It was always clear that the farmlands, located in this mountaintop village, inland from Minturno, south of Rome, belonged to her, and not to her husband, Antonio D'Arienzo. He was a bird of passage and used to say that America is like a whore — when you are away from her you want to go to her, and when you are there you can't wait to go home. Angela Puccia seemed to have spent most of her later years apart from my grandfather, who finally did return to Pulcherini for good when he was quite old and Angela had already passed away. The farmland and orchards with large lemons, the pigs that were slaughtered in the spring, the day laborers – all the things my father remembered of his childhood home – were always under his mother's supervision.

I never knew Angela Puccia. My father Camillo was fifteen years old when he come to America and left her and his two sisters, Camilla and Antonia behind. He came here in 1930 during the "height of the depression," he used to say – to join his father who was a day laborer living in Brooklyn. After working on road gangs for a few years, my father learned to be a barber and enjoyed his first flush of prosperity. He saved enough money to return to Italy to visit his mother and sisters in 1937. He stayed nearly a month and when he departed, he left behind everything he owned except one suit of clothes.

Several photos taken at the time of his visit show him as a tall, very slim, young man, with his mother at his side. My father and mother, Jennie (nee Giovannina) Del Vecchio were married in 1940 in Our Lady of Grace Church in Brooklyn. I was born in 1943. Did Angela Puccia know of my existence? Perhaps not. By then World War II had come to Pulcherini with a vengeance and the village was overrun alternately by German, American, British, Canadian, and Polish forces. The bombardment that accompanied the Allied invasion of southern Italy was all around, and later, the nearby monastery of Monte Cassino was obliterated. Eventually, Pulcherini and the surrounding towns were evacuated; the men were taken in one direction and the women were moved north to Rome.

Later, when the battleground had moved further up the peninsula, those who could, attempted to reclaim their land in Pulcherini. Angela remained in Rome, and when her relatives eventually went back for her, they were told that she had died. Apparently, she had eaten some food that was poisonous.

My cousins, Tony and Lisa Mallozzi, who were children when World War ll came to Pulcherini, but managed to survive and later prosper in the United States, remember Angela Puccia in the years preceding the war. She was a formidable, almost frightening old woman, who was often generous, yet fiercely protective of things that belonged to her. She especially guarded her fruit trees and when branches began to droop and sag due to the maturing fruit, she would walk around the trees and tap a stick into the earth directly below each to mark its location. This was her method of keeping inventory. When the fruit needed to be picked, she insisted that she alone should do it. But, she would always share the fruit with her family and neighbors – adults and children.

Although they lived through some very rocky times together, my mother and father generally were good friends and companions, especially during their later years after both my brother and I married and left them to themselves. But there was always one thing that they would fight about, right up to the end: my father would insist on shopping at the neighborhood's markets. He would travel through this area on his way to and from his barber shop — the bread store, the fruit and vegetable stand, meat market, and the pastry shop. When he arrived home with all his purchases, there would not be enough room in the refrigerator to hold it all. "You bought it," my mother would say in exasperation, "You put it away."

I have come to see that for my father, a full refrigerator was at once a remembrance, an atonement, and a victory over the deprivation and suffering and loss of his early years --- for those times when there wasn't enough to eat, for the times he and his father had no work, for the poverty of Pulcherini he had seen during his visit in 1937, for his mother Angela's careful counting of the fruit, and her control over its bestowal, for her own hunger and terror during the war years, for her dying alone away from her home and family, while her son and her husband were an ocean away.

The farmlands in Pulcherini now belong to my cousin Angela, who inherited them after my father gave them to his sister in 1956. I plan on seeing the fruit in the orchards very soon, and I hope that I will be there when the fruit begins to ripen.

Angela D.Danzi

∞ Togetherness ∞

I lived in a house in the East End of Utica, New York since 1948, the year I was born, three years after World War II ended, until 1955. It was nearly a one-hundred percent Italian American neighborhood. Surnames like Nattaro, Mamone, Papa, Ciccelli, Ianacci, Arcuri, Scala, Diorio, and mine, Danielle, were prominent. All the residents of my house were Italian American. The home had been built in the early 1900's by my grandfather and his older brother not long after arriving in the United States. It was a large dwelling in terms of the number of apartments it contained. Many buildings in the area had the same type of architecture.

Our building was a three story, flat roofed house that had eight apartments. The house was actually one apartment wide but three apartments deep. There were three apartments on the third floor, three on the second floor and two on the first floor. My grandmother lived on the first floor and occupied what would have been a double sized apartment. Grandpa, her husband had passed on years earlier. The eight apartments in the structure were definitely not up to 21st century building standards. For example, my family's apartment, on the third floor did not have running hot water. There was only one location for water, a cold water spigot at the kitchen sink. This same condition existed in some other apartments in the building.

As young children, my brother Tony and I took baths in galvanized steel tubs because the bathroom had no bathtub. On some occasions we bathed at other people's homes. My parents needed to take "sponge" baths or ask grandma if they could use her bathroom on the first floor. At times they would walk down the street to the public bath facility to bathe. When Ma required hot water for washing clothes or doing dishes, she had to heat water on the gas stove. It seems as if there was water continuously heating on the stove for some hot water need.

The apartment was virtually unheated. The stove, with a very small built-in space heater, provided heat for the entire four-room apartment. During winter we 'd close off little used rooms when they were not occupied. During the day when Ma was home alone in the kitchen, we'd close off the heat to the other three rooms. Sometimes the weather was so severe that ice would form on the inside walls of the three unheated rooms. Interestingly, because we lived on the third floor with a flat roof directly above us and with very little attic space, the reverse was true in summer. It was hotter than hell inside the apartment. However, because our location in the building was on the street side, we had the luxury of a large porch which extended across the entire width of the dwelling. This was where our family spent many a late evening sitting on lounge chairs awaiting a cooling breeze which, sometimes did not arrive.

Aunt Jane, my father's sister and her husband Tony lived on the second floor, directly below us. They did not have children. On the first floor below their apartment was where grandma lived. She was one of two sisters who married brothers; my grandpa and his brother. The four of them lived in the same city in Italy and were married there. Like my father, his brother had been deceased for many years. Also living in grandma's apartment was Angela, an unmarried aunt, my father's bachelor twin brother, Aunt Helen, her husband Stan, and their two young children. The apartments were not spacious but always clean as one would expect from immigrant homemakers in the 50's.

It may seem a bit odd that an extended family could have lived in near poverty conditions three to ten years after World War ll, but such was the case for me and my family. All of us in the dwelling, whether direct relatives or friends, managed to get along well. We enjoyed some meals together, shared pots and pans, a pound of flour, a cup of sugar, as well as "loans" of this and that. This togetherness was, actually, one of the most cherished remembrances of my childhood.

Vincent A. Danielle

∞ The Cinderblock Wall ∞

In 1950, my parents moved out of the Italian American neighborhood of Villa in the Bronx, New York and spent their life savings on a modest Cape Cod house in a new suburban community of Springdale, Connecticut.

The surrounding area was still largely underdeveloped. A small brook ran along side of our house. It was fed by two large cement drainage pipes that carried water under an intersection adjacent to our property. Four years later, following a very severe late spring thunderstorm, the pipes weren't able to accommodate the tremendous increase in water volume and the brook overflowed its banks and poured across the intersection, flooding our front yard.

Foreseeing the possibility of a future disaster, my father built a cinderblock wall around the entire perimeter of our property to protect our house in case of another flooding occurrence. He built it so strong that the foundation rested on a cement footing below ground of more than twelve inches thick with the wall extending above that point. When finished, the wall had a serrated surface. He then artfully applied a coat of smooth white cement over the entire wall. Yet, among the green lawns and white pickets fences of

Connecticut, it stood out. I recall one of our neighbors commenting on the Italian obsession with brick and building blocks.

In 1957, Hurricane Diane struck Connecticut with devastating fury, uprooting trees, washing away bridges and autos, and destroying homes - as was the case in Springdale. The sky was black for days and the rain never let up in its demonic intensity. The brook next to our house suddenly became a roaring river and the incessant rumbling of boulders swept up by the raging current prevented me from sleeping. A statewide emergency was declared, the National Guard was mobilized and finally we had to abandon our home to stay with hilltop neighbors.

As I stepped out the front door, the night we were asked to evacuate, I saw a river where the street had been that swept across our neighbor's property and emptied into the raging brook. I waded through the water that, by this time was up to my waist. I was terrified but held my grip on mother's hand. The current tugged at my legs and was trying to sweep me away into the cauldron of churning water and clashing rocks further down the road. As I plodded, I saw my father, in a frenzy of motion with his face shrouded in a floppy hat, piling up sand–filled burlap bags on top of the cinderblock wall that allowed our property to become an island. It was inundated on all sides by water.

When the storm finally stopped, we returned to our home. There were cavernous craters, piles of stones, and debris left in the storm's wake. The water had risen in our neighbor's house until it flooded the living room and bedrooms. Nearly all the homes in our colony suffered serious water damage. But as if by a miracle our home was spared. Except for some dampness near our basement exit door, the interior of the dwelling remained unscathed by Diane's destruction.

Forty years later, and long after my father had passed

on from a heart attack, I occasionally stroll past the house where I grew up in Connecticut. The modest Cape Cod has been converted into a hideous barracks-like structure by its present owners, but the cinderblock wall remains intact.

Gil Fagiani

∞ Dancing Behind the Glass ∞

Aunt Lilly sat resolutely in the rocking chair of our front porch on Market Street. Ironically, her name suggested a tranquility that was strangely at odds with blackjack wielding. Her real Italian name was "Pasqua," which, in English, means "Easter," but we called her "Lilly" after the Pascal flower because it was easier to pronounce.

On that particular day she took on a new role, not just as our aunt but also as our protector. The blackjack she held onto wasn't the slick metal kind used in gangster movies in the forties. It was brown rubber, arrayed with hairs like a golf ball suddenly let loose. Its shape matched exactly the head of its intended victim, Fritz Coleman, who swaggered confidently down the street toward our house. He had come to face my mother who accused his wife of consorting with my father on those nights he pretended to be washing the venetian blinds at the Fort Steuben Hotel.

Fritz appeared more like an actor out of character in a stage play than a suitable defender of his wife's name. He looked almost comic, in his yellow-loud salesman's suit, the one he wore to hawk meat in the cattle yards at two pennies a pound, a pound of flesh traded for his wife's broken vows.

My mother sobbed uncontrollably on the phone on the day she confronted Fritz with his wife's betrayal, but he reacted with denial, swearing to make her swallow her words. Now he stood at the foot of our front steps, facing Lilly primly seated in her best attire. Everyone in town knew Fritz was an "old cheater," and if it hadn't been my father with whom his wife had cheated, we would have felt he got his just desserts, never dreaming it would be at our expense. The irony of it was almost as painful as the day my mother took me to the Hub Department Store to confront Mabel Coleman in the very place where she and my father worked. Mabel, her blonde hair wrapped up in a smooth twist, remained calm and aloof through the ordeal. She reminded me of those old posters of Betty Grable and Lana Turner smiling smugly over their shoulder at the men who patted their behind as they jumped from planes.

Mother came unglued. Her words gushed out as Mabel stared down disdainfully, unmoved by her trembling voice. I didn't understand all of the words, but I knew that mother was in trouble. Mabel picked up the phone to call my father, who managed the second floor, but it was too much to face them together, and she was afraid of the look on their faces that would take away any doubt that the stories her friends were telling her were true. So we fled down the fire escape stairway, like angels cast out of heaven, too embarrassed by my mother's sobbing to take the elevator.

Now Fritz had come to our very house to make my mother take back her lies and accusations. I stood frozen inside the house behind the crystal facets of our front door, opened just a crack so I could hear. As he stumbled up the steps, Lilly showed no emotion or fear. No doubt he had a few drinks to bolster his courage, for his face was tinged with the alcoholic's pink mask, and perspiration stained the armholes of his jacket. When she saw him, Lilly began rocking back and forth in her chair until the moment he reached the top step. Then suddenly, as if choreographed in advance, she rose, gracefully raised her hand above her head, the blackjack clenched in midair, her step perfectly timed to match his approaching gait. "You taka one more step, and I'm gonna bumble your brains," she said in broken English.

Fritz stopped. He made no move and stood there on the porch staring at what must have crossed his mind as a very formidable woman. Maybe he was afraid of Lilly, afraid of losing his dignity. This was the 40's and one just did not physically strike a woman unless one was a rogue; and Fritz was no rogue. After all, he had come to defend his wife's name. I watched his face, a jigsaw of patterns behind the glass, saw his lips say something to Lilly, their voices an unintelligible garble. He shifted his hat into his other hand, animatedly pointed his finger toward his chest as if speaking of himself. Lilly's arm still raised, said not a word. He paused at the foot of the steps, and in that moment between movement and indecision, something must have crossed his mind. Slowly, he put his hat on his head, and backed down to the pavement. Lilly lowered her arm as Fritz turned and walked away down Fourth Street.

Whatever his motive for retreat was, we never mentioned the incident again. We just went on as we always did after some crisis, whether it was my father's obsessive drinking after the story became unraveled, or his running off with Mabel leaving the new inventory at the Hub Department Store a mystery for the owners to figure out, or Uncle Frank's untimely death of prostate cancer. The women in the family stood up under the blows of disappointment. They bought clothes on the time-payment plan, stared the butcher in the eye over an ounce of fat, and made our broken hearts whole again.

Years after that night, I would look back at a picture of Lilly and remember a woman, gray beyond her 47 years, a scowl on her face, and wisps of her hair in disarray. It was almost as if she were humoring the picture-taker, perturbed at being called away from the washboard where she scrubbed Uncle Frank's soot-covered work clothes. I would wonder when I looked back at that picture if all of the married women who came over from the old country let themselves age and go gray, surrendering their youth to marriage. Perhaps they took on this look of dowdiness, sharing in the eternal sadness of husbands who left behind the cool mountains of Italy to burnish with sweat the spikes of the railroad ties they pounded in place.

The evening after Fritz left, we went on with our usual household chores. Assembled in the kitchen, my mother washed chickpeas, my grandmother pummeled dough into pliant loaves and laid them into black iron pans, and Lily stood at the stove, stirring the basil into the dimpled kettle of fresh tomatoes popping their skins in the boiling water.

Marilyn Bates

Life's Lessons

The General

∞ La Terra Perfetta ∞

Tuscany has been called the "perfect land." For many people, Tuscany IS Italy. Romantic and poetic, it rarely disappoints: cypress line soft-edged Tuscan hills. The taste of its full-bodied Chianti wines and orange-roofed ruined stone farmhouses are enough to keep visitors spellbound. Tuscany remains a place of enchantment for me. Ever since my first visit twenty years ago, my private mission has been to convert all the first-time visitors I can to seeing Tuscany as I saw it. Even this statement sounds naive for I can never again see this place as I first saw it. The cities and countryside have altered in innumerable ways and so have I. Still I continue to attempt to recreate that perfect time. My devotion to Tuscany and Florence is no doubt linked to my youth. Back then, I held on to my Blue Guide and ticked off every portrait I could see in a week's time – most of which hung from crowded walls. Even the Florentines find their riches embarrassing and admit that Florence's art is the worst hung in Italy.

When I brought my husband to Florence for the first time during an early spring, he was bewildered by the maze of narrow streets and the shear volume of the detail of the city. He was still heady from Rome, the first big city he'd visited in Italy. I was crestfallen, but I found candidates to join me.

Not long ago, I returned with my husband again, with my two septuagenarian parents in tow. None of these family members had studied art history and I was now more than twenty years from those classes myself. What was more pressing to me, was the sense of mortality: although I was sure I would return, my parents might not be able to visit again. I wanted to be perfect and comprehensive. In spite of such ambitious standards, I managed to give them a sweep of Tuscany in three days. They didn't remember everything; at times they just kept thinking all of Italy was this beautiful and other times they remembered the waiter, a meal, a bargain, or a pizza that they didn't care for. But they also remembered the colors of its light.

We entered Tuscany by train from Venice. The visits to vineyards and hills remain with my father. "I remember the clarity of the water, the freshness, the sun." The sun didn't always shine – not even on that train ride – but it is the light in Tuscany that is the most recalled feature of its countryside. My father was impressed with the size of the Tuscan vineyards; miniscule compared to the farm fields in our country he once tilled and irrigated as a young man in the Civilian Conservation Corps (CCC), and as an agricultural student studying under the GI Bill. Tuscany is one of the few locations that still have forest areas that lure hunters to set out for wild boar or *cinghiale.* And when the chef (in this case, also the hunter) prepared it with the region's other resource, mushrooms, or *funghi*, the results are a woodsy combination of the wild side of Tuscany. For this is the only region in which to track wild boar – other regions, Tuscans laugh, domesticate their boars – no sport in that. Although I missed my sunny tomato sauces, raisins, and *pignoli* nuts left behind by the Arabs to sweeten meals in the Sicilian south, the game featured at the Tuscan tables was a treat.

Florence is not like Rome, bulging with magnetic masculinity and the power of its ancient ruins, nor is it perched in a fanciful setting like Venice with its closed alleys, secret cul de sacs and profound, eerie silences off the Grand Canal. Florence throws her head back, unembarrassed by her beauty. One of her main squares, the Piazza della Signoria is filled with gorgeous men, Cosimo, Neptune, and a copy of Michaelangelo's David.

Florence feels like a women's city. It is manageable in size; its buildings are not massive. Set alongside a river, she breathes and alters with the seasons, and her attention to detail is something many women can identify with.

Her name remains a mystery but no clear mythology points to the woman for whom she may have been named. Known as the center of the Renaissance, Florence's wealth was built on "the cult of the beautiful:" textiles, paper, gold trim, leather, and jewelry.

Vestiges of that age are evident in tables made of inlaid stone in large swirls and peacock tails based on Medici patterns. The elegant peacock motif decorates marbled paper, a craft that arrived from Venice; even the trite souvenirs bear a resemblance to the real thing. The Florentine leather curing process leaves animal skins more pliable, softer, smoother than you would find in any other place – it is also long lasting.

And while I wanted my parents and my husband to be able to stand in front of David transfixed, as I had once been and hoped to be again, I could not expect them to wait for three hours in the rain in a line that wrapped around the city. Nor could I expect them to do the same at the Uffizzi. This was time for a reality check.

I brought them to places where they would not be enveloped by the crowds, dwarfed by the volume of significant *objets d'art*. They had to be close enough to touch, ask questions, and bring not only memories, but also concrete evidence that they had been to all those places on our itinerary. If you were to begin and end your trip to Tuscany in Florence, it would not be the end of the world, just a reason to return. Before the long shadows fell across the hills, one late afternoon, we headed for San Gimignano; one of the best preserved medieval walled cities in the region.

Delle Belle Torri as it is called looks like a crown of

beautiful towers that creates an unmistakable skyline in the distance. Founded by the Etruscans, it was controlled by two great families who fought for a century. The only time they stopped fighting was during the Black Plague of 1348. Eventually, San Gimignano came under Florentine rule. Because the autumn sun was sinking quickly, we did not follow a formal tour, but sat in the Palazzo del Popolo listening to an impromptu concert complete with harps. Within the courtyard are preserved frescoes that include a Renaissance *chiaroscuro*. My mother and I stopped at a jewelry store that sold reproductions such as those sold in museum shops. At first, the proprietor spoke in careful Italian, but when she heard my mother address me in dialect, her face broke out into a full smile admitting that she too was from the south of Italy. She wanted to know more about where my mother was from. Nothing could have pleased my mother more than to be taken for a native.

When I ask my parents what they remember most about Tuscany, it was a little bit of Florence, the vineyards, the wines, the countryside, the colors, a trattoria, the food, but there was no mention of the Duomo or the Giotto frescoes or other wonderful art pieces we had seen. I reviewed our three- day itinerary; in between the lines to David and the Uffizzi, my husband did not see anything of any importance on this trip. I, on the other hand, was left with the impressions and vignettes that form a beautiful friendship that changes as we change, creating new paths to old places and new ways to visit a dear old friend with even dearer and older friends.

Maria Lisella

∞ A Letter to My Children ∞

My Dearest Children,

I want to tell you how important it is to be Italian, and what being Italian means to me. You are both old enough, my precious children, to consider what I have to say.

First, a small confession, and admission, if you will, for reasons I don't fully understand: your father is not all Italian. Just half by a standard commonly used. I am one-quarter Irish and one-quarter Swiss. Don't laugh or scowl. This is no joke, not humorous nor cruel. I'm not denying these other fine bloods, and this is no show of disloyalty to the United States, my cherished birthplace. Its just that I decided long ago to be Italian (Italian American, if you will). It was an important decision I made in my youth during a search of my roots. Then, as now, one hyphen was all I could bear, three were ludicrous and "American" alone simply was not descriptive enough.

It was a decision that had nothing to do with percentages of blood. That standard is even meaningless in Italy today, where bloods have been mixed and blended freely by a turbulent history. It had nothing to do with citizenship or loyalty to the United States, since nothing can shake that. Rather, it had to do with how I perceive myself and the heritage on which I elected to build. Being Italian was the dominating force, what I decided to be above anything else.

What about you, my little ones? You have the name, my curly headed boy, and I hope you will always keep it. You too, my round faced, dark, lovely little girl. You were born in Italy. But now your surname masks a half dozen bloods – the Irish, the Swiss, the Italian, and your beautiful mother, the French, the Syrian, and the Slovak. So what are you? Can you be all these things? Children of the universe, perhaps, citizens of the world, cosmopolitans, Americans, of course, but what else? Who else? I hope you will be Italian like your father.

Some of the most prominent Italians have been English (Byron and Shelly), so you needn't worry about the problems of blood and birth. What I'm talking about is a state of mind, an attitude, and an approach to life that, typically, Italians enjoy. Above all, to be Italian is to be passionate, to keep the burning fires inside you under control. Americans admire "cool" but believe me when I say that "cool' is overrated and frequently nothing more than a blank facade concealing stupidity, fear, indecision, and impotence.

Naturally, you must be bold. Challenge the dreams that dance in your mind, not recklessly, but with intelligence and skill. Emulate Garibaldi, Columbus, and Fermi in this regard, but also the millions of Italians who have traveled abroad as if to the moon in pursuit of a better life. Also, you need to equip yourself with a complete set of emotions. If you are to be Italian, you must master and use the nuance of every laugh – as your heart, mind, and soul dictate — and every form of sigh. Weep when weeping helps (even you manchild) and cry to heaven when all else fails. Read Dante and you will understand.

Be mafia-like in your loyalty and respect for parents, brothers, sisters, all family and friends. No other people on earth cherish the concept of family more highly than we Italians. Your uncles, Paul, Tony, Gerry, Dick, and Walter will tell you what I mean for I trust them with my life. Find your Bacchus, knowing first that he was Greek, thus the zest for living. After all, there is nothing like a good raucous and slightly out of control party, and a fine meal with family and friends. Pass the wine and the calamari.

Reach inside yourselves for the creative forces that you possess as surely as your eyes are brown. Find the genes and the genius that has given the world its finest art, its sweetest song, its most cogent argument for being – and express them as best you can. This will be hard work, the search for the Michelangelo, the da Vinci, the Verdi, and the Cross in you.

As you proceed with all of this, you have an obligation to please the crowd. They know that we are easygoing lovers, that we are capable of bragging, that we are actors on the stage. Try to be modest as you manifest these superiorities lest they stop believing. Use D'Annuunzio as your guide and the bewitching Eleonora Duse. I ask you, however, to set limits on these stereotypes. Love only those worth loving. Feign affection for no living thing. Forgive the innocent and demand punishment for the guilty. Let no man seriously call you any mean name, remembering your father's combative father in this regard. He knew that lovers have honor.

I have become too sentimental now. And so it is time to stop, short of that dangerous Italian point between sentiment and melancholy. Please be careful on that edge. I hope this letter has been persuasive, that it has helped you make the necessary choice. Somehow we must keep what we are alive through the generations of love and marriage. Find yourselves, and I believe that you will find the Italian that should be in every man born mysteriously to this life.

Kisses, hugs, and love,

Dad

Ernest A. Lotito

∞ A Lesson Learned ∞

One of the most outstanding and heartwarming memories that I still cherish is the celebration of holidays. Special foods for special observances, card playing (briscola and sette-mezzo). Family reunions were pleasures for all in an ambiance of festivities. My favorite time of day was when all had satisfied their appetites: the tables were cleared, wives and young women retreated to the kitchen to do the dishes and to engage in the latest gossip. Children all disappeared except for myself who lingered to enjoy "story telling time" by some of the men. Some of the stories were true from personel experiences, while others were handed down tales. But all had a moral, akin to Aesop's fables. My favorite recounts the story of a young man, Mario, the youngest of five children, two flighty sisters and two indigent, fun-loving brothers.

From early childhood Mario manifested mature propensities beyond his years. He would seclude himself in his room and study every book on a variety of subjects including literature and history. He would read them over and over again.

At a young age he worked in the vineyard with his father, tending the grapes and making the wine. His serious demeanor in many other pursuits and his refusal to join in their frivolities annoyed his brothers and sisters to such a degree that they termed him, *corpo morto*.

Mario's father was quite impressed with his son's mental inclinations and serious pursuits. Since none of his other children was interested in attending college, sending Mario was worth the financial sacrifice. But to the others he was still "corpo morto." They were glad to be rid of him. Following Mario's "summa cum laude" graduation, the father decided to celebrate the occasion by providing a special dinner for the family. A fat hen was purchased and roasted with all the culinary trappings. When the hen was cooked the mother set it in front of her husband who traditionally did all the carving. At this point, one of the disingenuous brothers wryly stated, "Let the maestro do the carving. With all his education he surely should be capable of that." The father hesitantly slid the dish to Mario who promptly picked up the carving knife and cut off the hen's head, which he placed on the father's plate. He turned to his father and said, "This is a respectful token as head of the family."

Mario then cut off the neck of the hen and placed in his mother's dish. "Mother, this neck represents you as the connecting link in the family. Without you there would be little or no communication between father and us. The size also represents the little appreciation shown you by the family."

Next the legs of the hen came off. Placing one in each of his brother's plates he explained, "I am giving each of you a leg because you are always on the go. No destination, no goal, just a meandering, listless time-wasting lifestyle of no return."

Finally the wings of the bird were cut off. Placing one in each of his sister's dish he stated, "These wings go to my sisters who are here today but will soon fly away to another self-indulgent activity." Scanning the astonished faces around the table, Mario proclaimed, "Now what's left?"

Of course, a corpo morto. Therefore, by designation, pointing to the remaining hen, "This is my domain." Picking up his knife and fork he proceeded to carve the remainder of the hen. Then as a respectful son would, he first passed the plate to his father, followed by his mother and then back to him. The three of them enjoyed the meal, in full, while the others stared in envy.

Upon completion of the meal Mario rose and turned to

his siblings, "Corpo morto no longer exists, never did." He picked up a few of his mother's home-baked cookies and retreated to his room.

Following this story, there was a brief exchange of remarks among the men listeners. Then another story was recounted. And so it went for more than an hour. Following the completion of the last tale, the women came into the room with playing cards in hand and the games began.

From these sessions I learned more about human nature, character development, and life styles than is written in many psychology books.

Most of our parents lacked a formal education as we know it today, but they more than made up for that lack by being constantly inoculated and exposed to applicable proverbs and sayings handed down from generation to generation and proven by the test of time.

Joseph M. LaPorta

∞ Its Time to Go Home ∞

Domenico Fodaro was my Calabrese grandfather. He came to America when he was a young man of seventeen years to try to earn some money to send home to his family. While here he learned the trade of shoe repair. He worked very hard and eventually was able to open his own shop. He loved the work, which he was very good at, and enjoyed it until he was eighty-six years old. Everyone with whom he interacted loved him and his work. The repair shop stood solid and unchanging for more than sixty years, even as the area went through all of the evolutions and changes through which city neighborhoods had suffered, becoming home to one ethnic group after another.

"Pop," as he was called, was the center of this changing community because he really loved its people – the people of America. He was so grateful to be in this land, and to have the opportunity to make a living. He often handed out shoes to the poor – free, and bought soda pop for the kids who passed by his shop and greeted him. He chatted happily with neighbors, old and young, and anyone who would listen. My grandfather was the epitome of the theme song, "God Bless America," land of *abbondanza* and the idea that a person could "come from nothing"to maybe becoming president, one day.

Although his love for America was apparent, I often sensed a longing when he recounted his nostalgic tales of Italy and lovingly remembered his hometown of Girifalco, provincia di Catanzaro. Year after year he unfailingly sent money and shoes to his *parenti,* especially to his sister Maria, his last surviving sibling. He would frequently look at a picture of Zia Maria that he always kept close at hand. She resembled him but was petite and dressed in the ever present black. In contrast, my grandfather was stout and although his Italian conscience demanded he wear a shirt and tie even when relaxing around the house, his clothing was unmistakingly and more colorfully *Americano*.

One day, I convinced my loving grandfather, in my beige suit, straw hat, and buck suede shoes, to return to Italy with me, to see his sister at last. Fifty years had passed since they last saw one another and he had recently lost his wife, my grandmother. He found himself thinking more and more of his homeland. I felt that a trip back in time would make him feel reconnected to life and to family. He often spoke of "going back," wanting to finish his life in the land in which it all began. That sounded logical to me. We decided to make the voyage.

Why was I so certain that a person who is separated from his motherland would always be willing to go back? Reculturation, I thought, had to be somewhat like riding a bicycle. Can you ever forget how to be *Calabrese*? Yet the interaction that I observed between Pop and his place of birth was not what I expected.

A short time after we arrived in Calabria, we made our way down the bumpy dirt road together, conscious of our awkward "foreigner" appearance. The glares and stares of the townspeople in their black and brown clothing made me feel slightly out of place, though it didn't seem to bother Pop. We reached the home of Michele, one of grandpa's nephews, where the outpouring of affection that followed was almost surreal. My grandfather, for all his years of loyalty and devotion to his roots, was treated like royalty and I could tell that Domenico Fodaro was doing quite well with the showering of attention. I would say it did him well – at least at first. The cousins made sure that we were comfortable, had good food to eat, and were updated on everyone's details. Later in the day we walked to the home of Zia Maria. She greeted us with arms flailing and with tears of joy, occasionally dabbing her eyes with the apron she was wearing. She latched on to her brother, my grandfather, and hugged him for what seemed an eternity. The two were overjoyed with their reunion.

As the days passed, however, I noticed that grandfather seemed to be more and more restless. In the 70's, Girifalco was a place that stood still in the face of time. The Italian dialect of the town was not as my grandfather remembered it, and the old ways and customs, which should have been welcomed and familiar, were no longer his own. Although showered with all the love and affection that the town could muster, his heart was no longer solely Italian. The revelation for us all was that he was equally American. It wasn't, after all, a lifelong dream to return to his roots, but a lifelong dream to recall his roots – that was the essence of his heart.

Of course the family begged him to remain with them, and although his love for them was unmistakable, he didn't hesitate for a moment in his reply.

"No it is time for me to go home to America. I have family there, and a business to look after," he stated in all seriousness. "I miss my little house and the attached shoe shop, and the ethnic neighborhood where I live."

He embodied the Italian American concept. He was kind, proud and happy, a lover of life, music, and people. He was a businessman who worked hard and made something from nothing. And from our memory of Pop, we all learned something we could never have learned if the best of these two cultures had not been combined before our eyes. We learned what it meant to be Italian American.

Raeleen D'Agostino Mautner

∞ The General ∞

My father died when I was thirteen years old, in the early 1930's during the Great Depression. As a result, my mother immediately became head of a household which consisted of nine children whose ages ranged from five to twenty-one years. One would suspect she needed to be quite a disciplinarian, so much so that we called her, "The General." The kind of punishment she meted out was almost as severe as that which I received later in life, as a member of the armed forces.

I really felt sorry for my three sisters. They had very little freedom. They were allowed to date only if they had first reached the age of eighteen – even then they could not date often. Before any of my siblings, boys or girls, were allowed to date, they had to bring the date home to be interviewed by "The General." It was embarrassing for all of us to sit and listen to the "interview" before she gave permission for the date to occur.

For my sisters, this was not the end of it. I recall when my older sister, at eighteen, was allowed to date. She had to be chaperoned. That job was given to me. I was sixteen at the time, and I really didn't mind. It was common during the 30's, in Italian families, that when a daughter began dating, she usually married that first date. On this occasion I was not concerned about any bad behavior between my sister and her date, and I knew that my future brother-in-law would flip me a dime and tell me to get lost for a few hours. I never really got lost, I just kind of moseyed along at a fair distance from the dating couple. The dime just assured that I would provide a good report to "The General." I did, however, fail to report that they held hands and sneaked in a short kiss or two (as if "The General" didn't know).

The boys had a lot more freedom. I could not go out on evenings of a school day, but on weekends, I was allowed to attend a movie with my friends, go bowling, or attend a chaperoned church dance. Of course with each of these outings came a curfew which I was expected to observe. None of us owned a key to the house so I was usually on time. "The General" possessed the only key. She also had the safest security system in existence – the slide bolt. If any of us came home late we would have to knock on the door. She'd get out of bed head for the door, and slide the bolt to the unlocked position. As I entered, she'd be standing in the doorway swinging a large wooden pasta spoon at me. I laughingly dodged the spoon, gave her a kiss on the cheek, and dashed off to my bedroom while she sternly yelled, "You Bum."

She was "The General" all right and if she could see all of her children today, I think they would all say, "Thanks Ma."

Joseph Mileo

∞ Pa, the Disciplinarian ∞

In 1946 I owned a 1938 DeSoto four door sedan with a new Dodge truck engine in it. The engine was purchased through the transportation company for whom my brother worked. The engine was installed by my brother-in-law, Sam Mesolella who was, truly, a master auto mechanic. I was twenty years old, single, and living at home with my parents. I had a full-time job, turned over my paycheck to Ma each Friday evening and received a five-dollar allowance in return. Pa didn't know how to drive, although I tried to give him driving lessons several times. He always froze behind the wheel during the lesson because he felt there were "too many cars on the road."

I liked my car very much and so did my parents. I ferried Ma and Pa wherever they needed to go during the day or early evenings, while I had the car to myself on weekends. It was both a luxury and a necessity for all three of us.

My personal curfew during the week was 11:00 P.M. and on weekends it was 1:00 A.M.. At times, when I had difficulty meeting these time constraints, especially on Friday and Saturday nights, I would definitely be in deep trouble with Pa. However, I had a list of excuses for being out late.

"Gee Pa, I had a flat tire."

"I ran out of gas."

"One of my friends got sick so I had to drive him home."

"I lost track of the time."

"I temporarily lost the keys to the car."

"I left the lights on and the battery went dead so I needed a jump to get it started."

Very often my reason for staying out beyond the curfew was because I owned the only automobile in the large group of guys I hung around with which meant that, sometimes, I had to make two trips to wherever we were headed for the evening.

On several tardy occasions, I'd park the car along side the house, tip toe up the steps to the side door, turn the key slowly, and enter the kitchen. I immediately removed my shoes because I needed to sneak, as silently as possible, past Ma and Pa's first floor bedroom. I prayed that I would hear two people snoring, not just one. But, there was always that squeaky board in the dining room floor that signaled my late arrival.

Pa awakened at the first squeak, and in his long flannel sleeping gown and bare feet, confronted me. With fingers fully extended on his right hand he raised it to his mouth, bit hard in the area of the forefinger, and vehemently stated, "What's the matter with you. Don't you see what time it is? Don't you know its late. We were worried about you. Maybe we should take the car away from you. Other boys don't stay out this late. You gotta go to church in the morning. Maybe we should make you come home earlier."

This tirade lasted for the better part of half an hour without interruption or interference on my part. After he finished I told him I was sorry and that I would respect his curfew from that moment on. That was it. Pa never held a grudge, didn't mention the incident again. I padded off to bed. It was past 2:30 A.M.. I slept soundly that evening. Similar incidents would repeat themselves about once a month.

Edward Albert Maruggi

∞ Mannaggia L'America ∞

Being the last of four children born of immigrant parents, I did not learn to speak or to understand the Italian language. While I could not translate what was said, I was able to figure out the emitted emotions: happy, sad, critical, frustrated, humorous, etc.

One day, in the early 1940's when I was less than ten years old, I was with my mother at the neighborhood corner grocery where she was speaking in Italian to the proprietor. The dialogue was firm with the usual Italian hand and arm gestures providing emphasis. I felt that the emotion displayed was that of criticism, and the topic was about America. During their conversation I occasionally heard a certain expression that I knew always meant a criticism of American culture. To this day I hear in the echoes of my mind what I think are the words, "mannaggia l'America, I had no idea and still do not know the precise meaning of that phrase.

Upon returning home, I asked my mother, a woman to whom I *always* spoke to respectfully.

"Ma, if you don't like this country, why don't you move back to Italy" I said uncomfortably.

She gave me a stern look. She was obviously annoyed and responded in her heavily broken and accented English.

"I donta wanna to returna to Italy. Justa becausa you criticisizes a country, donta mean you no love it."

That lesson in good citizenship was to stay with me throughout the social unrest period of the 60's and 70's. Each time I saw on TV an act of protest by the citizens of this country I heard that maternal voice in my head say, "Because you criticize a country doesn't mean you don't love it."

Because of the education my mother gave me that day on how to be an American, I have always seen civil protests as the right of a people to speak out about the country they love.

Vincent Ortolani

∞ Crossed Fingers ∞

My son and I returned to New York after living in Italy for nine years. Andrea had attended *la quarta* (fourth grade) in Naples, and since I did not want him to lose two years of schooling (he started first grade at the age of five) in the American public school system, I immediately enrolled him in *La Scuola d'Italia*. It was a bilingual school associated with the Italian Consulate in New York City. There the courses were taught mostly in the Italian language with the exception of an English language and culture course. *I professori*, as they were called, were Italian, usually doing a five-year stint at the school. While much of the school and most of the teachers were progressive, one of the teachers had a curiously "old fashion" disciplinary system, and Andrea was quickly learning some "Americanisms," from some of his *amici americani,* like crossing one's fingers when lying. The merging of the two cultures made for an interesting encounter. Upon picking up Andrea from school on this particular day, he appeared to be a little more animated than usual. Nearly out of breath from running towards me he stopped at the car and blurted,

"Mom, guess what? My gym teacher punished me today. He told me to go to the corner of the gymnasium and said I should stay there, on my knees."

Of course, like any good Italian mother, whose own mother would always ask what I had done to offend the teacher when I got into trouble, I asked the same of him.

"What did you do?" I said. He responded defensively,

"Nothing much. I pretended to be a sports commentator while some of my friends were playing soccer. Mr. Oliveri wasn't pleased, so he told me to go to the corner and remain there on my knees until class was over. After a little while my knees hurt so much I got up a few times. He came over, pushed me down and smacked the side of my head when I kept complaining."

I must explain that soccer was Andrea's favorite sport. When he sat on the sidelines, either because it wasn't his turn to play or because he was told to come out of the game, the frustration would drive him to do a play-by-play analysis of the game, much to the dismay of Mr. Oliveri. Even though this was when most parents would complain about any physical liberty taken with their child, I did not. I had attended Catholic school at the time when a smack on the side of the head was nothing to complain about. So

I just asked my son to behave and to give the gym teacher a break.

I thought that would be the end of it. Andrea was a good boy and very rarely gave me anything to worry about. He was just a bit mischievous at times. About a week after the incident, I asked him how gym class was going. His response brought two reactions: anger and laughter – anger at the teacher's actions and laughter at how seriously Andrea had taken an old American superstition. Seems that Andrea had told Mr. Russo, his homeroom teacher about his gym teacher's behavior, and as a result the gym teacher was reprimanded. Obviously, there were going to be consequences. The soccer game was the main activity of gym class, and at the next class the game would pit the fourth grade against the fifth grade. Andrea was excited. He was a very good player who would jump at every opportunity to play, but Mr. Oliveri had something else in mind.

Just before the teams were picked prior to the start of the game, Mr. Oliveri approached Andrea and angrily stated.

"Mr. Russo has told me that you said I hit you. You know that's a lie. I cannot tolerate anyone who lies and little boys who lie cannot play in this game."

Andrea was devastated. His friends were watching and waiting for him to be picked to play. He knew his team would easily beat those fifth graders, and couldn't wait. He thought for a few moments, placed both hands behind his back, crossed his fingers and said apologetically.

"You're right Mr. Oliveri, I am very sorry."

He played in the game, and the fourth grade won handily. After hearing the story, I was furious. Andrea with a puzzled look said,

"Don't worry, Mom, I crossed my fingers so the lie doesn't count."

The next day I headed over to the school and spoke to both the gym teacher and the Headmaster. As a result, there were no more such incidents in gym class. But Andrea was still perplexed. He knew that lying was wrong, but genuinely thought that that simple act of crossing his fingers would erase the lie. After all, *i suoi amici americani*, as he repeatedly emphasized, had told him so. But now he also knew that it didn't work. He had learned a lesson, Mr. Oliveri had learned his, and I learned my own. Times had changed, discipline methods had changed, and the student was not always to blame. Next time, I wouldn't ask,
"What did you do?" But rather,
"What happened?"

Rose De Angelis

Celebrations

The Italian Wedding

∞ The Flying Angels ∞

My grandfather was a member of an Italian men's organization whose annual duty was to march, carrying the marble shrine of the Madonna, which weighed a ton, in a procession ending in the piazza between the church and the school. At some height above the piazza, twin wire cables were strung between the roofs of the church and the school. I was involved in a plan to dress two young children; a boy (me), and a girl in satin angel outfits, complete with haloes and each carrying a basket of rose petals for this festive event. We were to be suspended by these cables. The criterion for child selection was that members of the men's club must choose them.

This event took place at night. At the precise time when the shrine arrived in the piazza, while loud fireworks were exploding in the background, we began our descent from the roof of the church. We started reciting prayers in Italian beginning with, "Silencio, Silencio." Adding to the chaos of the event, several infirm people were being lifted to the shrine directly beneath the cables, affixing paper currency to the passing Madonna. There is an apparent legend of dubious veracity regarding the origin of this ritual, which supposedly follows the loss of the Madonna statue in Sicily and its miraculous appearance on the shores of the New World, in remarkably good condition.

So now, the shrine is in the piazza, at rest between the church and the school, fireworks are popping off, cripples are effecting miracles —- assembly line style, while two unrehearsed children in angel costumes are precariously harnessed to twin cables high above the piazza The crowd of gesturing and screaming Italians was yelling as we began to lurch into the abyss of darkness, which was suddenly illuminated by the lights of the stands and booths, vending pizza, nuts, beef, and games of chance.

As we were being lowered on the cables I was, at six years of age, seized by vertigo which led me to drop my basket of rose petals on some miracle seeker, and forgetting my prayers in Italian. Instead, I was concentrating on my hysteria. This alerted the little girl angel to her identical predicament and she matched me with a pathetic theatrical display.

The rest is a dim memory, including the disappointed and furious demeanor of my grandfather who was waiting on the opposite roof where I had unavoidably landed. I had brought shame upon him and his organization for which he never reproached me, although that night he did not speak to this disappointing event.

Many years later, as an adult, I was on a trip to Great Britain. My tour included a visit to the tower of Saint Paul's in London. I was climbing the countless steps to reach the top when the height induced the identical reaction of many years ago. I was forced to go up and then down the tower stairs before I had an opportunity to pass out --- frightened, teeth chattering, perspiring profusely, and remembering why I had not worn satin since I was six years old.

Frank Morreale

∞The Saint Joseph's Table ∞

There are many saints whose birth dates are honored throughout the annual calendar which are celebrated by Catholics as well as by Italians. By far the most popular one in my neighborhood was a "table" honoring Saint Joseph. Saint Joseph was very special to my family as well as to all Sicilians. He is the patron saint of Sicily and is also my namesake.

This popular celebration had begun many years ago by the people of Sicily to show gratitude for the rains that came after a very severe drought, thus avoiding a near famine on the Island. The people in the various villages rejoiced because their crops were saved; their prayers had been answered.

To remember Saint Joseph, each year since then, on the anniversary of his birth, most Italian Americans of Sicilian heritage still prepare a table with a special assortment of foods, primarily vegetarian in nature (baked goods made with flour, fruits and vegetables). My family was no exception.

Each year on the nineteenth of March, the birth date of Saint Joseph, my family celebrated this event with an open house event. It featured an enormous buffet table of fresh fruits and vegetables, fish dishes, homemade pastries, and many, many loaves of freshly baked bread. Our parish priest personally blessed the bread. This celebration was a daylong affair with neighbors, friends, and relatives visiting; some staying for a few minutes while others stayed for hours. Some people brought additional food to share with others, but each family left with a loaf of bread that the good reverend had made holy. Leaving with food was the symbol of food being distributed to the poor of Sicily.

Today, many of the tables are given to thank Saint Joseph

for favors that have been received during the previous year while other tables are given as a request for a special intention.

Joseph Mileo

∞ An Italian Thanksgiving ∞

For years, celebrating Thanksgiving at Aunt Betty's was very special. It was a traditional get together of family. Always friendly and happy, Aunt Betty and Uncle Tony were also gracious and hospitable. The host and hostess as well as invited family members all took part in the feast.

Grandma Marino made the eggplant, baked a la parmesan, and also cold in a salad. My parents supplied the pies, one pumpkin and the other a fruit pie. Uncle Joe and Aunt Nancy brought the wine, homemade of course, and a variety of nuts. There was always the "token" turkey. After all, this was an American holiday. The trimmings included bread and giblet stuffing, cranberry sauce, and sweet potatoes. But the main course was homemade lasagna or ravioli made by Aunt Betty. It was so good; most of us had seconds.

Crusty Italian bread added a nice touch to the meal. I don't recall who furnished the bread, but it was always fresh. The salad contained various types of lettuce, carrots, garbanzo beans, bits of celery, tomatoes, and onions. Uncle Joe's homemade vinegar and extra virgin oil added to the salad made the meal nearly complete. Along with the pies, espresso and coffee were served, often with a touch of homemade anisette or sambuca added. The final course included an assortment of cheeses and fresh fruit.

As we were all stuffed at this point, it was time for us to retreat to the living room where Cousin Anthony played the piano and my brother John and Uncle Joe strummed on their guitars. We sang Italian country songs as well as American folk tunes. It was truly a warm and loving experience with family. We certainly had a lot for which to be thankful. Thus, Italian heritage and customs were added to the American holiday.

Richard Marino

∞ Jesus, Mary, or Magic ∞

Baptisms in the Roman Catholic Church are often seen as a social event and a display of various cultural beliefs. As a Roman Catholic priest, I have the opportunity to experience many of these. Although, at times it becomes a struggle between faith and culture.

Recently, at our parish of Saint James, we were preparing the after Mass Baptism of Antoinetta, a new born. As usual with an Italian baptism, the families were not at Mass and so we had to wait for family and friends of the family to arrive. At the outset, if was difficult for me to find Antoinetta in the flowing and full white baptismal gown she was wearing. I finally located her little head sticking out; however, it was adorned with a hat full of lace and veils. It seems that it had been previously worn by her grandmother. That's all well and good but the hat had to come off. This was a Baptism and it might get wet. After some discussion, I convinced the parents that if they didn't remove the hat it might be ruined by the water. As long as they could put the hat back on immediately afterwards, for photographs, they would be happy.

Then the big problem arose. Antoinetta was wearing a gold cross, a gold Miraculous Medal of Mary, and a gold cornu (a pepper shaped horn) around her neck. Since this was a Baptism, I politely asked the family to remove the cornu from around baby's neck. That is when grandma yelled, "NEVER!, NEVER!" I indicated to her that the cornu was a superstition and that it had no place within a faith-filled sacramental ceremony. She did not care. She was not going to budge. Then she enlightened me,

"It is to fight off evil," she said. I proceeded to tell her, forcefully, "Jesus is the one to fight off evil."

"If Jesus dying on the cross doesn't work then we have Mother Mary, and if she doesn't work, then we have to depend on the cornu."

In frustration, I told her and the family that if the cornu was not going to be removed, there would be no Baptism. After much more ado, I was able to proceed with the christening. Immediately after the Baptism the hat and the cornu went back on, and photographs were taken with each relative.

I have not seen Antoinetta or her family in church since that day. I guess the cornu isn't fighting off evil but fighting off faith. Wait, they will be here in a few more years. That will be time for Antoinetta to receive her first communion.

Reverend Michael M. Mancusi

∞ La Festa Madonna del Carmine ∞

Preparations for this feast always began long before the opening night. During the first week of July the children's street play was interrupted each morning at ten by village workers who lazily erected the wooden posts that supported thin bridges of tiny Italian lights that hung overhead. Although the only area of town that was affected by the Feast was a two block square section with the Church of Our Lady of Mount Carmel at its center, the whole town could feel the approaching festival.

Signs announcing the event were displayed in all store windows. Lake Street traffic would slow at Twenty-third, the main boulevard of the Festa, as drivers peered down the street to check the progress of the workers. The front yards of the homes on the parade route were cleaned by their owners and strung with lanterns and tiny Italian lights. Statues of the Madonna were adorned with fresh and plastic flowers, and candles in tall red, yellow, blue, and green glass cylinders.

The closer to the night of the Feast, the greater the activity in the neighborhood, and the later people would stay out in the streets. Even Paci the popcorn man kept his little popcorn truck open later than usual. The open windows of the homes without air conditioning sucked in whatever breeze the evening offered along with the melancholy sounds of Paci's plastic piccolo. Two nights before the opening, striped tents were erected over wooden frame stands on Twenty-third Street and the street was closed to all but Feast traffic.

In the cool, early hours of opening day, the carnival arrived. After working through the dark morning, the elaborate rides and game stands appeared to the waking eyes of the children who lived near the church.

But the morning of the big day did not stop routines. Fathers went off to work with their silver lunch pails to the factories, brown bags to the family stores, and briefcases to the offices. The milkman hired a helper for the week and made deliveries earlier than usual to accommodate the increased orders for milk, cream, ricotta cheese, and ice cream. The produce man, in his green painted, converted old school bus, slowly cruised down the streets, ringing his thick dull bell at every house calling out,

"Watta-malones, pepperoni, frutta, verdure, cippole. Come anna see watta I gotta fo' you," in between the bell rings. The junkman coasted through the alleys in his rusted flatbed 1950 Ford truck,

"Rags an' ol' iron." It sounded more like "Ragsaline, Ragsaline."

Down the sidewalks strolled the knife sharpener man, pushing an old wooden wheelbarrow he had converted into a portable sharpening shop, calling out,

"Sharpa, sharpa, sharpa knife, makea, makea gooda wife. Bringa you scissors anna knife to me. I willa make 'em sharpa you see."

But for the children all the usual games were postponed as they wandered through the streets watching the blond-haired carnival characters ready their stuffed animals, their floating ducks, their lead bottomed milk bottles, and their mechanical rides.

By noon, the hot summer air steamed with sizzling sausages that cooked slowly over hot coals. White aproned men and women prepared troughs of sliced beef, sausages and peppers for the evening. Village workers stopped at the various stands to talk their way into a free sandwich. Priests and nuns hustled their way in and out of church in their black garments, preparing the altar, and a circle of old women in black surrounded the statue of the Madonna that would be carried through the streets on Sunday. In a field, a few blocks from the church, carpenters were busy building the stage that would hold a portable altar for the outdoor Mass. Through the haze of charcoal smoke and steam from the cooking beans, that would be sold in glassine bags, workers hurried to ready the area. Civil Defense trucks that would become portable first-aid stations moved into position.

This feast has been part of Melrose Park, Illinois since 1894, but is origins were not important to the children and teenagers. What was important was that the festival changed the whole character of their town. For one week, people who were grouchy would grow friendly. Those who usually stayed indoors would come out and be a part of the crowds of celebrants. Former residents of the town returned to Melrose Park for the festival, feeling the same tug that others might feel when returning home for Christmas. The Feast was a common point of reference, like a yardstick for measuring the changes in friends and relatives. For years since the Feast had started, very little about its celebration had changed. But people had changed.

The holiest of men could be seen crying out for people to lay their money down for a chance to win a carton of cigarettes, a kewpi doll, or a cut glass goblet, to bet on what hole a mouse would run into while it spun a flat roulette-like wheel. Old women in black who daily huddled in church, with their hair tied tightly in buns, could be seen, white strands of hair waving in the air as they danced the *tarantella* in the streets, singing in loud voices. It was the one week that those who had hidden their Italian heritage the rest of the year would proudly display it in public. For the teenagers, the Feast was a magical time that took a sleepy town and dressed it in colored lights and lured thousands of people to its streets for a week. It was a time when curfews were not enforced and gangs of boys acted like newly appointed deputies. If someone new to the area looked like they were ready for trouble, the boys would chase them out of the area. If any of the carnival hillbillies got smart with one of the local girls, the boys would surround his stand or ride, and taunt him to fight. If he were fool enough to fall for the taunts, his stock of stuffed animals, other prizes, or even his money would quickly disappear.

Most of the men waited in line at the "Ring the Bell with the Sledgehammer" game, in sleeveless t-shirts, trying to impress the women with their strength, or at the "Knock the Negro in the Water" game.

How this poor black man was talked into sitting in a cage and taunting the throwers with, "Hey Mistah Spaghetti, you can't knock me in the water," or "Hey dago, you can't knock me down," no one knows.

The owner would stand in the crowd, pulling guys by the arm and coaxing them to drop a quarter for a chance to knock this poor guy into the water. He'd yell out,

"You, you, here's your chance to soak a shine."

"C' mon, give! This guy needs a bath. You can do it."

Each age group had its own location. Old people sat in chairs along side the church, away from the crowded streets, watching people pass, commenting on the length of the girl's dresses and amount of makeup on their faces. They'd sit there and talk about how the Feast had changed over the years and how the intent of the *La Festa* was completely lost. The young children ran around near their grandparents and were yelled at in Italian if they strayed from grandpa or grandma's sight.

By nine o'clock, the light on the streets would come from yellow bulbs with rusted tin hats that swung from wooden posts and the colored streams that shot out from the amusement rides, and orange rays that flayed out from under the wooden cooking stands.

Most evenings of the Feast had a moment at which they would peak and then it would be down hill to early morning and home. Often the peak came with a fight: chasing hillbillies out or gangs fighting a dishonest gametender. By ten o'clock the pace of the Festivities picked up with the families heading home. Some stopped for a last cannoli or lemonade; children bought their last bags of lupini or roasted chick peas, and old folks stopped for a last prayer before the doors of the church were closed for the night. By midnight only the police would remain on the deserted, littered streets. By the time the sun rose the next morning, the streets would be spotless and ready for the next night of the Feast.

Fred L. Gardaphe

∞ The Italian Wedding ∞

In the forties, when I was growing up, one of my fondest memories was that of attending an Italian wedding reception. In the Rochester, New York area, this celebration was usually held in a "hall', i.e. The Labor Lyceum Hall, The Fraternal Order of Eagles, The Realmonte Hall, on the west side, the Caltanisseta Hall or the Valguanera Hall on the east side of town. The wedding was always on a Saturday with the reception held early that same evening.

At the reception, guests were greeted by the bride and groom at a long table located at the back of the hall, near the stage or bandstand. The table was usually covered with a white tablecloth. Sitting on the table in serving trays were homemade cordials, such as creme de menthe, anisette, strega, and the like, made by one of the wedding couple's parents, as well as homemade cookies, and "favors." Favors or "confetti" were little white candy covered almonds wrapped in a white netting and tied with a thin white ribbon. They were provided to the line of guests as they approached the newlyweds. But the most important item on the table was a neatly wrapped or decorated box with a slot on top. This was for *la busta,* (the envelope) a monetary gift for the bride and groom. The amount of money placed in the envelope usually depended upon how close the relationship was between the guest(s) and the newlyweds' families. For example a *comare* or *compare* (Godmother or Godfather) would, in all probability, give the bride and groom a larger amount than a neighbor.

Folding chairs, often borrowed from the local funeral home, lined the perimeter of the hall. They were three or four rows deep, for guests to sit. Plates of peanuts in shells and homemade cookies on trays, and sometimes ham sandwiches were served out of a large clothes basket. It took two people to carry the basket when it was full. Beer in large pitchers and pizza were brought around to the sitting guests as they watched dancers doing *la tarantella* and other traditional Italian dances while the accordion-led orchestra played traditonal Italian favorites.

A special part of the celebration took place near the end of the evening when guests lined up for servings of the multi-tiered wedding cake and baked goods from a large Italain cookie tray. The cookie tray was round in shape and consisted of eight to ten layers of many different kinds of cookies including almond paste cookies, miniature custard cream puffs, macaroons, cookies made of multi-colored dough, and chocolate covered ones. Some had an alcoholic flavor.

The most popular song for the special dance for the bride and groom was, "I love You Truly." During this waltz, adults as well as children wrapped so many streamers around the dancing newlyweds that when the music stopped, the couple had great difficulty separating from one another. By ten o'clock the bride and groom had left to begin their life together at a local hotel before leaving the area for their honeymoon.

    I always dreamed of having an Italian type wedding, but by the middle nineteen fifties, the typical wedding reception format had changed. My parents insisted on a buffet dinner served at a local party house because it was the "in" thing. No peanuts in their shells, no homemade cordials, no beer served in pitchers, no ham sandwiches served in a clothes basket, no live music, no pizza, only a disk jockey playing records. Oh, well!

Roslyn Piazza Smith

∞ Christmas Is ∞

Love,
Family, dear ones, friends,
Affection, joy, happiness, comfort, peace,
Superb music, delicious food, bright decorations,
Children, family stories, reliving childhood experiences,
Religious rituals, devotions, praying... Il Presepio,
Anisette, special wines, friendly drinking,
Torrone, Panettone, pranzo con nonna,
Joining youth and age, rich and poor, saint and sinner,
Nostalgia, gladness and sorrow, pleasure and pain,
Forgetting, forgiving, forming closer relationships,
Select words, an embrace, fond glances, caring,
Introspection, self-inventory, planning,
Parties, shopping, gifts, sharing, visiting,
Remembering those not present, a tear,
Discussing special parental traditions,
Redesigning goals for the New Year,

A white blanket of snow covering the remains
of summer,
Focusing the life cycle.

Joseph J. Bentivegna

∞ Holiday Celebrations ∞

The Advent season was a particularly auspicious time of anticipation among Italian immigrants. Today's custom of writing and sending Christmas greeting cards was unthinkable among Italians one or two generations ago. A family might send holiday greetings to a few relatives or friends in Italy – picture post cards with a Nativity or religious scene, and a brief message such as *Buon Natale, Buona Festa, or Buon Capo d'Anno.*

However, for most relatives and close friends near or far, it was almost imperative that sometime during the holiday season, one made a personal home visit to exchange greetings. During such a visit, guests would surely be offered a glass of homemade wine or cordial made from bootleg alcohol flavored with anistte, strega, or creme de menthe. The alcoholic beverage was usually accompanied by some form of homemade baked good, such as *calzoncelli* (literally, small pants) stuffed with ground almonds, filberts, chocolate, and cinnamon. Another favorite was *taralle*, cookies in the form of loops glazed with frosting. Yet, another baked delight were honey-dipped fritters in the form of small wreaths.

As children we longed for a traditional Christmas tree with the customary ornaments, tinsel, icicles, etc. But my father and mother promised us something more beautiful and meaningful —- a Nativity creche or *Presepio*. During a

Christmas shopping spree they purchased, at a store that sold religious articles, a set of statuary figurines including the Holy Family, shepherds, sheep, wise men, camels, and stable animals. My father then constructed a stable in the form of a cave to house the manger, infant Jesus and the adorers. For ground cover, moss was dug from nearby woods, creating a beautiful and natural setting. Over a period of years the Cappiello's *Presepio* was admired by countless friends, relatives, and well wishers.

The vigil of Christmas was awaited with special anticipation because it was celebrated as a religious day of fasting. The evening meal usually consisted of a *minestre* of greens (dandelions, escarole, or endive), followed by angel hair pasta with meatless marinara tomato sauce, and several varieties of fish – capitono (large eel), anguilla, (small eel), merluzzo (whiting), or baccala (cod). The common beverage was my father's homemade wine. Later that evening the adults prepared for and attended midnight Mass at the parish church.

On Christmas day, it was my mother and sister's task to prepare dinner that usually included home made ravioli containing ricotta cheese in an tomato sauce. They also stuffed two chickens which were oven-roasted in a pan with wedges of potatoes and vegetables, and flavored with vinegar–preserved round red peppers.

Appetizers consisted of tender stalks of celery and fennel which enhanced the flavor of the red wine. When the various dinner courses had been served, if appetite and space permitted, a special Italian holiday dessert was available – *sanguinaccio* (blood pudding). This delicacy was made of hog's blood ordered by our favorite local butcher, from a slaughter house. The recipe calls for a mixture of hog's blood, whole milk, bulk chocolate, and cinnamon. These ingredients were heated in a large kettle and allowed to simmer for nearly half a day, requiring constant stirring, in only one direction. When the mixture thickened sufficiently, it was poured into pie crusts and allowed to cool. Unless a novice actually tasted the delicious flavor of this pudding, he or she would be a little reluctant to eat it. However, once sampled the old expression, "the more you eat, the more you want," definitely applied, despite the rich and high caloric intake.

Joseph Cappiello

∞ An Almost First Communion ∞

As is true within most Italian Catholic families, a child normally makes his/her First Communion at the age of eight. This is known as the age of reason, when a child is supposed to know the difference between right and wrong. First Communion is a very important sacrament. This is the first sacrament that follows that of baptism, which normally takes place shortly after one's birth.

Ma enrolled me in a First Communion preparation class. As it was planned that I was to "make my communion," at Holy Family Church, she signed me up to take the class scheduled from two to four every Sunday afternoon at the parish school, for a period of ten weeks.

However, Sunday was the day that I was given a weekly allowance by Pa. My allowance was eleven cents; ten cents for the Murray Theater and a penny for candy. I eagerly looked forward to going to the movies every Sunday afternoon with my friends. It was not uncommon for us to sit through two or even three full double length feature performances (nine hours of movies), plus Movietone News, and a serial movie of some type. Even though the movies started at 1:30 in the afternoon, my sister

Edith had to come drag me from the movie house once at 11:30 PM.

After the ten-week period of First Communion preparation classes had concluded, a teaching nun from Holy Family school came to our door one evening. She had come to inform Pa and Ma of a very grave matter. I recall being home at the time of Sister's visit.

"Your son Eddie will not be making his First Communion with his class this year because he failed to attend any of the scheduled preparation classes."

"Eddie," Pa asked angrily. "Why didn't you attend any of the classes Ma registered you for?"

"I went to the movies every Sunday afternoon, Pa. You gave me an allowance every week so that's where I spent the money," I reluctantly admitted. Even before Sister left the house, I was reprimanded and scolded very severely, by Pa.

The thing that really surprised me about his reaction was that he was not a religious person and only attended Mass on Christmas Day, Palm Sunday, and Easter Sunday, or at funeral Masses for deceased members of *La Societa di Melfi*. But, I suppose he wanted to show Sister what a good parent he was. I promised him and Ma that I would religiously (!) attend all of next year's classes. So I received the sacrament of First Communion the following year at age nine. I did not skip any classes. I went to the movies on Saturday instead.

Edward Albert Maruggi

∞ Sorry Tony ∞

Every year, on a long weekend around the middle of June, we have a feast in our parish celebrating the anniversary of the birth of Saint Anthony of Padua. On the Wednesday through Friday prior to the feast there is a tridium of prayers and benediction at the church. On Saturday evening there are food tents and beer booths and a wine garden. There is also a large stage set up for the band to play and an area for dancing as well. All of this takes place in the parking lot behind the church.

For some reason the music and the singers seemed extra loud this past year, several decibels higher than usual. The parish telephone began ringing at 8:00 P.M., with calls from neighbors complaining about the noise level. Even the police had to be called three times. I spoke to the family in charge of the festival and their only response was, "*mezzanotte.*" I couldn't allow this to go on 'til midnight!

The police indicated to me that the town ordinance states, "outside noise must cease at 10:00 P.M." At ten that evening, I was still in a very heated dialogue with the family to stop the music. It finally stopped at eleven, but then came all the announcements. As it turned out the microphones were "on" until mezzanotte.

There was a large group assembled on Sunday afternoon at 3:00 P.M., as we were ready to begin the Rosary procession around the church property. It appeared that no one could follow directions. What was most distressing was that the people responsible for the procession couldn't even get the order correct. Banners were in line where statues should have been and visa versa. Nobody was following the right group of marchers, and to make matters worse, the band was playing loudly in front of the church.

The best, however, was saved for last. Four young men

were enlisted to carry the statue of Saint Anthony in the procession. In the church, two long wooden planks were placed, horizontally, under the table-top that held the statue. But, the men forgot to unfasten the legs of the table prior to carrying the statue out. I was so afraid that the statue would begin to teeter and yelled to the young men to unfasten the legs. I could visualize Saint Anthony falling to the marble floor and crumbling before my very eyes. They slowly walked backwards to the original location of the table and unfastened the legs. I'm glad they didn't trip.

After all the marchers were in line, the procession started to move forward while singing a song to Mary, the mother of God. I didn't recognize the song because it was in the dialect of the family sponsoring the feast. But as usual with Italian feast days here, the procession got all messed up; people stopped when they should have been moving, stopping and moving, until various groups meshed with one another.

Every year I dread the season of Italian feasts. It is a time of mass confusion, too much drinking, too much eating, too much loud noise, and no one really knowing what anybody else is doing. Poor Saint Anthony, he must not look forward to our celebration of chaos.

Reverend Michael M. Mancusi

∞ The Missing Madonna ∞

They cancelled the feast after eighty-one-years
no more ragtag bands blaring martial music
no banners of saints flapping in the wind
no trembling hands touching the silver Madonna
just a big intersection smelling of incense
and a parking lot covered with weeds.

Gil Fagiani

Special Relationships

Uncle Larry's Funeral

∞ Gone, But Not Forgotten ∞

I grew up in an era long gone but not forgotten. My family lived in an Italian neighborhood among our relatives, commares, compares, and close friends. Sunday was such a special day for us. We all attended Mass at Our Lady of Mount Carmel Church on Woodward Street on Rochester's East Side. After Mass, neighbors and friends would come to call and we'd serve them homemade cookies, coffee and meatball sandwiches. For Masses on Saint's days and religious holidays there would be a procession with a band playing and with the congregation following.

On Saturday or Sunday nights, we usually gathered at a neighbor's house where men played their accordions and mandolins and we sang Italian songs and danced to the music. The women pooled their food, such as baked macaroni, sausage, meatballs, chicken, eggplant, roasted peppers, pizza, salads and baked goods. What a feast!

Our neighborhood was not without problems, like the day when a group of boys were playing baseball in the alley off Woodward Street. Chick Castronova was up at bat. He hit a long fly ball that crashed through Mrs. Pelligrino's kitchen window. After a few seconds she came roaring out her side door, her apron covered in red. Chick was terrified, he thought it was blood. She grabbed him by the collar and shouted,

"Your baseball landed right in the kettle filled with my tomato sauce and it splattered all over me." She yanked him by the ear.

"Come with me, I'm taking you to see your father. I think he should know about this."

Chick's father owned a neighborhood meat market a couple of blocks away, on Scio Street. Upon arriving at the store, Mrs. Pelligrino explained, with an emotional tirade, exactly what had occurred. Mr. Castronova listened patiently to the baseball incident, then placated her with a pound of ground beef for meatballs and a couple of cans of tomatoes for her sauce. Everyone was happy and Chick would go on telling this story for several years at every opportunity.

We did not have material things but we had fun, love, and friendship to last a lifetime. The old neighborhood as I remember it, may be gone, but it is not forgotten.

Teresa Marino

∞ The Old Neighborhood ∞

It is painful recalling the poverty and the struggle for survival in the old neighborhood during the early days of the depression, which in the early thirties included a smattering of Italian, Irish, and German families. This was the east side of Rochester, New York. My father died when I was very young so it was Ma's responsibility to hold the family of eight children together. We always managed to have food on the table, how, I'm not really sure. We didn't have much money so Ma had to find bargains and sales whenever she went shopping. She found that the best deals were right in our neighborhood. Most of our household needs, for example, could be purchased within two blocks from where we lived. We didn't have an auto, who needed one? Fresh fish, packed in ice, was obtained from a peddler who came by with a horse and wagon. Once a week the iceman came to fill our ice box with a fifty-pound block of ice. The Prudential Insurance man also came once a week to collect ten cents for each of the life insurance policies on the family. What fruit and vegetables we did not pick from our garden or those of neighbor's plots, we purchased from a man with a wagon selling these items. Every morning, the milkman delivered three quarts of milk and butter when required. Even the man who had a small cart with an emery wheel attached to it wove his way through the neighborhood to sharpen saws, scissors, and knives. Bread was baked at home. Ma and my sisters did the darning and patching of clothes.

My mother was also able to shop for my three sisters trousseaus without leaving the neighborhood. She purchased sheets, pillow cases, napkins (biancheria) from a Jewish peddler with a cart with two large, wooden-spoked wheels. He also sold curtains, and drapes, always careful to keep these items covered so that the sun would not affect the colors in the fabric. It was always amazing to me how my mother would communicate with this man who spoke both Yiddish and Italian and Ma responding in either language, as well. I lived in this environment through my high school years. It was quite a different world for me when I started college.

Joseph Mileo

∞ Corona's Little Italy ∞

The Little Italy community of Corona is located in the north central section of Queens County, New York City, surrounded by Lefrak City, the Long Island Expressway, the old World's Fair site, and Shea Stadium. Since World War II, the core of the Italian American neighborhood has changed slightly. In Corona today there are large pockets of Italian American neighborhoods with their support services of delicatesssens, markets, churches, senor citizen clubs, social clubs, funeral parlors, bocci courts, restaurants, pastry shops, and VFW. Godparenthood (*comparaggio*) continues as an important cultural practice.

Corona had originally been home to Germans, Swedes, Irish, and English, and a large concentration of Italians up to 1950. After 1960, the African American population reached 20 percent. Today, people from the Caribbean and Latin America predominate. But the most recent census data reveals that the central community of Corona is essentially Italian American.

My mother was born in 1904 at Prince Street in Manhattan's Little Italy. Her parents were born in the small village of Alvito, Frosinone, Italy. They migrated here around 1900 to live in Corona. My father was also born in Alvito two years before mother and migrated to the United States during World War I. He first lived in Harlem, then in Brooklyn, where large numbers of Italians resided.

When they married in 1927, my parents purchased a small two-story frame house on a large plot of land in Corona. Here my father planted several varieties of fruit trees, erected a grape arbor and planted an assortment of vegetables, while teaching his sons valuable ecological lessons. In late autumn we would rake up fallen leaves and bury them in soil that had been tilled. We also gathered horse manure from horse droppings in the street to be used as fertilizer. A balance of nature prevailed. Careful pruning of splendid gardens produced wonderful harvests. Underneath one of the three garages on the property was a cool area used as a wine cellar. My father was a wine maker.

The Italian language was spoken in the neighborhood, however, my parents did not speak it to their sons at home; perhaps it was their intention to hasten the assimilation process and to prove their patriotism during the war. Italian cuisine predominated, and my mother frequently disdained American cooking. Briscola was the most popular card game played. Money that my brother and I earned from part-time jobs had to be turned over to my mother. My father built a bocci court on the property. As a general foreman with the W. J. Barney Construction Company he hired many Italian immigrants to work as laborers, to help them establish themselves in their foreign land. They appreciated this gesture of friendship and showed great respect for him as their boss.

I attended Public School 14 in Corona where my mother had graduated. It was racially and ethnically mixed. Peaceful intergroup relations were the norm as all individuals played, worked, and studied together. We respected our teachers for their authority and erudition. Our parents supported the teachers in their daily role of surrogate parents. The public school system had a leveling effect on us, but it also weakened our immigrant culture.

During World War II we lived close to my father's mother, uncles, and their families. The family members were interdependent, assisting each other whenever possible. The usual predictable feuds prevailed among us, eventually to be resolved, only to rise again in newly shifting family alliances.

We were neither poor nor rich. My father often stated that he never lost a day's work during the Great Depression. He could not understand why Americans failed to find work in this land of opportunity. He often showed concern over the growth of the welfare state. My parents voted Republican at the local and national levels. My mother worked as a seamstress before she married, but assumed the role of permanent homemaker as she raised her family. When her mother and father died in 1935 and 1940, respectively, her assimilation accelerated.

My father made certain that his two sons would go to college because he firmly believed education was the most effective way to move out of the blue collar class and to achieve the American dream. He always prided himself on this accomplishment. My brother and I were the only people in our immediate Corona neighborhood of that generation to receive a college education. Both of us did benefit from the G I Bill of Rights, but even if there had not been a governmental subsidy, we were expected to attend college. In fact, my undergraduate education had been completed before I entered the army during the Korean War in 1952. Moreover, the general attitude of disdain for education in our neighborhood often angered my father.

The Italian American population in Corona remained stable during this period. Ethnic strictures dictated that you marry within your own group. The binding tradition of *comparaggio* furthered the insularity of the community. Young ladies learned homemaking skills that were useful in marriage. When boys completed their high school education (some failed to), they immediately sought positions with New York City as policemen, firemen, or sanitation workers; jobs that were quite respectable and secure. We were a close-knit community and we showed it by visiting each other's homes to pay our respects, especially during holidays. The family was the strongest institution with parents maintaining tight control over children. Divorce was unheard of, nor was it practiced. Moral principles, Catholic doctrine, and social pressure kept families together.

In 1952 I married a non-Italian women from Corona whom I met in Newton High School. After two years in the army, we settled in the Long Island suburb of Plainview to raise a family, and to continue my graduate studies. Moving from the Italian American community of Corona to a more diverse, less densely populated suburb limited my contacts with the Old World culture. However, the formation of the American Italian Historical Association, and its regional chapter enabled me to participate in ethnic activities at a different level. My social network now consisted of intergroup secondary relations. World War II produced a greater tolerance for Italian Americans, which made it easier for me and my generation to succeed.

It is true that there has been movement out of Corona by some who have adopted more assimilative traits in the half-century following World war II. But the phenomenon of ethnicity has demonstrated that as newer ethnic groups have located in the larger area, and external pressures have been exerted on the perimeter, a substantial number of Italian Americans here preferred to remain in the core neighborhood. Here they can still practice and maintain the cultural traditions of their parents and grandparents, traditions that have been modified by time and the host society.

Even though massive Italian immigration ended over seven decades ago, Corona now embodies the classic Italian American community surviving profound social change at the conclusion of the twentieth century. While older Little Italys in New York City's sections of Mulberry Street and East Harlem, Chicago's Near West Side and Boston's West End and North End, may not exist today or may be skeletons of the past, Corona, as a microcosm of a Little Italy, continues to be a vital ethnic community within a much larger geographical area inhabited by many different people.

Frank J. Cavaioli

∞ Grandma ∞

Nana, is what we affectionately called my grandmother. She came to America on the steamer Champagne in 1900. She brought her daughter and my father, a baby hidden from public view. My father was her first born in America. She and grandpa settled in Columbus, Ohio. In Italy they left behind two sons who would later join the family here. She gave birth to four additional children, all daughters – in Columbus. Some years later, the family moved to Buffalo, New York. Nana was a very special woman to me as she was the only grandparent whom I ever really knew. All the others passed on shortly after my birth. My father died when I was only nine months old. But my mother was very close to Nana and together they showed what love and family are all about.

Since her parents were deceased, Mom considered Nana as her mother. Their relationship was like mother and daughter. Being a widow herself, Nana identified with my mother who was left with three young children. Nana made us feel so important in her life. All of her grandchildren were given unconditional love at all times.

Once in a while on a Saturday, Nana enjoyed making *polenta*. When the invitation was offered, we came running. There is nothing special to me about corn meal, but polenta was something else – sliced and coated with butter and sprinkled with grated cheese – or polenta balls stuffed with delicious mozzarella cheese (fresh from the oven), or maybe polenta chunks with tomato sauce and chicken livers. We never really saw her when she was cooking, but she sure added a lot of love. Whatever way she made it, we ate it. It didn't take long to get to grandma's house because we only lived a few blocks away and a good daily walk was important. Walking to grandma's house is a lost art in this day of automobiles. We looked forward to a visit with her. It was like singing, "we're going to grandma's house, we're going to grandma's house, we gotta get there, we gotta get there, we're going to grandma's house."

On certain occasions, such as a trip to visit her daughter in Sonyea, New York, Nana made her special mashed potato pie. On holidays, she made ravioli, her favorite recipe, one that included a spinach/meat stuffing. Just a sample was worth the wait.

Nana worked at the Statler Hotel as a kitchen laborer in Buffalo and once in a while she would bring home to us crispy Parker House rolls (we called them "pillows") that she had baked at the hotel. She wrapped them, along with butter, in a linen napkin and carried them home in her large handbag. Sometimes before eating them, we topped them with powdered sugar.

As a small child, I felt that Nana had a special place in her heart for my widowed mother and her three children. Being a widow with young children, Nana understood my mother's needs to keep her children close. It was a must every Sunday afternoon that our family walk over to visit grandma. Upon leaving her house, each of the three grandchildren received a kiss from Nana and she tucked two pennies in our hands. On Christmas it was a nickel. How surprised and grateful we were. This, from a woman who worked so hard, earned so little, and kept so little for herself. When she retired from work in 1941, she received a letter from the Social Security Administration advising her that she would now begin to receive twelve dollars every month. I still have that letter in my possession.

The end came for Nana on Valentine's Day in 1950. With her went all the recipes, which no one yet has been able to duplicate, as well as her gentleness and unconditional love. It was fitting that the Lord quieted her with a severe stroke while attending Sunday Mass as the choir was singing a hymn in Latin. She passed away two days later. Memories of Nana will live on as long as we allow them to. She never knew her great-grandchildren, but all her grandchildren were the luckiest people on earth.

Gloria A. Sartori

∞ Una Buona Femmina ∞

Throughout her marital life, my mother, whose formal education ended after the eighth grade, was convinced of several inexorable truths: she kept the cleanest home and she was the best cook and the hardest working woman in town. She was the shrewdest handler of money and the cleverest bargainer in the market place and would tolerate little nonsense and apologize not one bit for her expansive temper. She protected and loved her family in unsurpassed fashion and enforced the family code. She responded to her children's transgressions with her weapon of choice, the wooden spoon. Her children would go off to school only if impeccably groomed and she could double-guarantee that her children would someday graduate from college.

These are not latent truths. My mother often explicitly stated them, sometimes humorously, and even more frequently exemplified them with deeds. She challenged all family members to provide even one shred of evidence against her claims. None of them ever could. Her truths were unassailable. By the time she was forty-six, my mother suffered from an especially debilitating form of rheumatoid arthritis. By the time she was forty-nine, she was withering and confined mainly to her chair or bed, She died at sixty-two.

Was mother a victim of the pernicious southern Italian

patriarchy? Was she an illustration of the stolid virtues of a better time? Was she a feminist hero? The answer to such questions is plain. She was all of these things in part, but she was none of these things completely.

Mother was a victim of the pernicious southern Italian patriarchy: denied formal education because of economic necessity and gender, she was regarded by her generation as valuable mainly insofar as she ably fulfilled reproductive and domestic functions. She was viewed by the earlier immigrant generation as less valuable than a man and prevented by familial and social circumstances from sampling a healthy portion of the individual-community continuum.

She was also, however, an inspiring example of virtues less prevalent today. She harbored no illusions as to the prospects of her upward socio-economic mobility or of her personal, as opposed to familial, happiness. Instead she perceived herself as part of a wider subjectivity, as a link in a generational chain that stretched from Sicily to America. She understood clearly that her generation would never be fully American, but enthusiastically accepted the challenge of guaranteeing that the next generation, her children, would fully enjoy the bounty of the new world. This guarantee, however, could be realized only through her enormous personal sacrifices and unwavering commitments. She relished the challenge. She persevered during a period when the call for "family values" was not a hackneyed political slogan, but instead defined a way of life.

Mother was a feminist hero. Once her children began school, she ventured into the public arena and secured a job. Given her limited formal education and work experience, it was not surprising that the position she obtained required merely repetitious clerical tasks conducted in the cellar of a local tree nursery. From all reports she performed these tasks with distinction. Thus she combined job and family without compromising the demands of either. My mother did this, and more, without complaint and without resort to support groups or psychological counseling. She was a cultural transformer without public renown. More important, throughout her life she steadfastly refused to embody the moods and demeanors typically assigned to women. On the contrary she energetically, even fiercely, resisted patriarchal authority, especially when that authority jeopardized the family's well being.

When my mother died in 1980, her daughter was a tenured school teacher of mathematics and her son was a student at Harvard Law School. The dream had been realized.

Raymond A. Belliotti

∞ Uncle Larry's Funeral ∞

On the way to Holy Sepluchre, a Rochester, New York cemetery, our auto snaked through Seneca Parkway next to the Genesee River gorge. Driving, my father turned to glance at the unending procession of headlights trailing behind us. He paused and stated in wonder, "Look at the cars Larry's got." The procession filed in and parked along the neat and unending rows of marble and granite. It was Monday, December 27, two days after a solemn Christmas.

Uncle Larry was a permanent part of every Sunday of my childhood at Grandma Vaccarelli's pink stucco house on Avery Street in the city. Didn't everyone go to their grandmother's house on Sunday? And every holiday and birthday was spent together. My aunts, uncles and cousins were there faithfully, along with the food. The bready pizza with chunks of tomatoes and oregano sitting in the shiny oil. The *cardoones,* dipped in flour then fried in oil and egg; the irresistible *tarralles,* hard crunchy breadsticks flavored with fennel.

And every Sunday there was always Uncle Larry. He easily intimidated my cousin Laurie and me; a loud Italian like my father, small in stature, but round and strong. His hair was black but graying, with a monk's bald spot. Dark shadows lurked under his eyes, and his teeth were stained yellow by the pipe which for years he clenched between his teeth, off to one side, while he talked. The certain aromatic smell of smoke from a pipe instantly conjures up my grandmother's kitchen and my uncle. The family, uncles, aunts and cousins would congregate in the small kitchen. The room would become extremely warm so that even in midwinter someone would open a window. The whole lot of us would be talking and laughing so loudly, that Uncle Larry would eventually bellow, "There's this whole house and everyone has to be in the kitchen!" Full of expression, he would exclaim in Italian, pipe clenched between his teeth. He would growl, *Madonna,* then bite his leveled hand; or shrug his shoulders and swipe the back of his hand out from under his chin in a stiff motion. We kids would spend hours running around the house, the backyard and the basement, in and out of conversations and laughter. The aunts, uncles and cousins sat in the kitchen or in the backyard conversing about the latest news and old times, always with humor. We always laughed at each other's antics. Afternoons into evenings were spent telling us stories of their childhood during the Great Depression

Larry was the oldest of six; Aunt Toni (Antionette, or Neenat), Pat, Anthony, Tommy and Angelo (Ange). Ma raised chickens and rabbits in the backyard. When the milkman's horse-drawn wagon went past their house, they collected horse manure for their enormous backyard garden. Uncle Larry always came to our house in the country in summer to pick dandelions and cardoones. He played in the neighborhood with the man who was the owner of the Ragu Tomato Sauce Company, and with Aldino Cataldo Magiulli, who invented some kind of bathroom cleaner and became a millionaire. He told stories of World War II, baseball and boxing greats like Rocky Marciano, and always spoke with reverence of the music he loved, the Big Band sound.

We would listen to the talk, each brother adding his own perspective, while my grandmother and Aunt Mary spoke quietly to each other in Italian. Often, one of them would pause and begin, "Ma," and ask a question in Italian. I remember feeling left out, the language being almost as foreign to me as the stories of their era. Uncle Larry always told us about the time when he was in the army during World War II and had a military leave at Christmas time. It was Christmas Eve and no one knew he was coming home. The bus dropped him off at the corner of Avery Street and Lyell Avenue so he had to walk about three blocks home. The snow was falling gently in large flakes, sticking to his uniform and duffel bag. He was the only one on the street, and it was so quiet and so still that it was almost holy. Pausing in the driveway of the house and observing the glow of lights from the windows, he could feel a lump in his throat. As he walked through the door, the whole house was surprised, and my grandmother embraced him, crying.

Uncle Larry had a great passion for learning which led him, in his fifties, to learn to play the piano and return to college to earn his degree. He married our now Aunt Cloe. He organized every annual family picnic and Christmas party with a zest for involving us in games and activities like the egg toss, water balloon toss, and rope pull. He dressed as Santa Claus at the Christmas parties. Before my time, he would play games with the kids at grandma Vaccarelli's house, lining the kids up for a spelling bee.

His wake, along with everyone else who passed away in the family, was at the Bartolomeo Funeral Home. A lot of people I didn't recognize crowded into the room to pay their last respects to Uncle Larry. I had to wait in line to get to his casket. I've always been uncomfortable with the custom of kneeling before the casket. And now here lay my uncle, who shouldn't be dead from cancer at such a young age. Out of respect to him, I cross myself and kneel there, just thinking of how much I hate it. Half of me wants to look and see what he looks like dead, and half is sort of repulsed to be so close to a stiff, dead man. To say that it is difficult to comprehend his absence does not really express his loss from our family. I was a young woman and a piece of me, of my heritage, had just permanently vanished.

Two weeks before was our last family Christmas get-together with Uncle Larry. The once healthy, animated man had become so small and weakened. His voice, which could bellow over all our voices combined, had become raspy and faint. That Christmas was at our home in Riga, a suburb of Rochester, New York. The usual familiar hum of the entire Vaccarelli family was in the background and I knew this was the last visit with him. I took the time to sit next to and talk with Uncle Larry on our sofa. Someone so real to us, yet something intangible that made us who we were, was about to leave our grasp, and I had to be near this familiar, still alive man at this familiar, festive occasion.

Here and now, it is not sorrow I feel but a lack of feeling. I think of the flower arrangements; red and white roses, multicolored carnations, flowers I recognize but don't know their names. How their fragrance still reminds me of funerals. How I don't like certain laundry detergents because they have that same funeral flower smell. I think of the cruelty that only a month or so earlier Laurie's grandmother was laid out in this very same room. Uncle Larry came to pay his respects and everyone was surprised that one so close to death would show up at a funeral. I felt that it was dignified, yet I couldn't deny the strange feeling that I was watching a man who was in that place between life and death. Kneeling there still, I noticed the American flag folded in a triangle on his casket. He looks good despite the disease that killed him, but it doesn't really look like him. It's as though something essential is gone from what made him. Everyone kept saying, "He looks good."

Getting up to let the next person pay his respects, I watched my Uncle Tommy shrug his shoulders, throw his hands forward in a very familiar manner, and point out, "He looks good? He's dead!" There are two, short, round old ladies dressed in black mourning dresses seated in the back of the room. No one knows who they are. We asked my Aunt Toni and even she is not sure. It's the running joke at Uncle Larry's funeral, "Maybe they're the hired mourners." I am introduced to an aging Italian man, shake his smooth, soft hand and find out that he is Aldino Cataldo Magiulli.

Holy Apostle's Church is the huge stone edifice located at the corner of Lyell Avenue and Austin Street. It hosts Uncle Larry's funeral. It is a good Catholic Church; vast, full of echoes, cold, still, with stained glass windows, and merciless wooden pews. My favorite part of this familiar Catholic ritual is when the priest lights the incense in the brass jar with the holes in it, swings it back and forth while ceremoniously clanking the chain against it, spreading the pungent, spicy smoke which rises, accompanying Uncle Larry's soul to Heaven.

We pause, transitioning from the warmth of our cars to Holy Sepulchre, and pull our coats around ourselves against the late December cold. I admire row upon row of magnificent, elaborate stones; holy centurions made in various images of Christ, the Blessed Mother and winged angels. Each section is surrounded by old, towering trees. It was lovely, blanketed with silently falling snow. I remember, with an ache, the story of Uncle Larry coming home at Christmas time and of the softly falling snow in giant flakes. It wasn't wind whipping, frigid, driving us away, but, covering, muffling; it felt sacred, appropriate. I remember Emily Dickinson's, "After great pain, a formal feeling comes." We walk toward where the casket waits suspended above the neat, rectangular gap in the ground; the blackness all the more magnified by the contrast of the white snow. People are already standing around it, the funeral director is waiting to say the last words, near a pile of white and pink carnations for Uncle Larry.

My brother Donald, his wife Kim, my sister Sue and I slowly make our way to the spot. We comment to one another while watching the antics of our cousin Sherry and her mother, Aunt Marlene. They don't wear boots, but high heels in the snow. They wobble and progress like fancy, squawking flamingos through the snow. My brother wears a long, formal wool coat, which he borrowed from his friend, Mike. Sue says, "Nice coat, Don," and he replies, "Thanks, it's Uncle Larry's." At this, we all pause for a millisecond, as though someone threw a wrench in our thinking. "Uh, I mean, it's Mike's." But we're laughing. "Don!" Kim backhands him. He didn't mean to say it, and it's not appropriate to be laughing, but it was so weird and funny. In his own dense way, my brother articulated the strangeness, the displacement we were all feeling.

Finally, we all stood around the casket, around Uncle Larry, and formally laid him to rest. Rather, we said our final goodbyes and left him for the cemetery men. It seemed to me like leaving Christ for Joseph of Arimathea. My grandmother Vaccarelli's stone lay not far off, so some of us made our way through the fluff, and around so many other peoples' final resting places, to her and grandpa Vaccarelli's resting place. They have the risen Christ on their stone. I remember when I was a little girl (and my parents still do), we visited the cemetery once or twice a summer to plant flowers on the graves. Then, it was for those I barely knew; a precious angel brother gone before I was born, a vaguely remembered grandparent. It was something we always did, like going to my grandmother's house on Sunday's.

This day, I was vaguely concerned that Uncle Larry would be cold. I knew that after the burial ceremony we were going to my cousin's, his daughter's house for casseroles, a deli tray and jello molds. The family would gather around in our usual groups and most of us would end up in the kitchen, but today probably not as loud or with as much laughter. It's not the same at all anymore.

My grandmother's house was sold long ago, and that feeling of expecting to see Uncle Larry at family functions faded somewhere along the way. Most of us see one another now only at Christmas and the picnics. I can't help but feel that I wish I had listened more closely to his stories, because most of the details are vague in my mind, shoved far back into a dusty room, obscured by the needs of my own growing family. But always, I find a familiar, intimate comfort in soft, new falling snow, and in my memory rests a clear image of a man, and the excitement of asking, "Uncle Larry, tell us about the time..."

Carol Ann Vaccarelli Kinch

∞ Keep the Wheat and Let the Chaff Lie ∞

There's an old pair of shoes
resting on the extension ladder
in my garage. A pair of black Florsheim
wing tips, now scuffed, worn down to the heel
white paint splattered across the tops,
the lining of one torn and curled, the other missing.
They've been nesting on that ladder since 1980.
Twenty years I've cleaned that garage, spring and fall.
Forty times, I've returned them to their perch.
My Papa's shoes. Once proudly polished,
preserved with metal shoe trees inside.

Papa never bought sneakers or casual clothes
When his good clothes wore, he used them to
work around the house or yard. Once, he'd been
depression poor. Lost his house and sun-kissed fig tree.
Later, he spent money on beef roasts, schooling
for his children, books and bikes for my babies.
Throwing out old clothes, buying new ones for work
a frivolous waste.

These shoes he kept in my garage
along with frayed dress pants
a faded oxford shirt, a torn sweater.
He'd walk five blocks from his home to mine
impeccably dressed, not to embarrass me
before my neighbors. This gentle man
immigrant with broken tongue,
former farmer, friend of grape vines,
olive trees, and sweet, black soil
displaced in a city.

He'd change clothes in my garage
sweep the leaves from my winding drive
nourish my azaleas, with cow manure,
weed my favorite flower beds
plant forsythia and hydrangeas he'd rooted
make my house and yard look loved,
richer than the houses of my neighbors
whose hired gardeners manicured their lawns.

No one is perfect.
My mother had stories.
My older brother too.

Mother used to say
"You don't know your father.
Once, he ripped his custom made
silk shirt in two because he lost a
button, and us with no money."
My older brother'd say about my parents
"When I was a boy, they'd go at it."
He'd shake his head.

But I know none of that.
I remember him legally blind at 80,
gently lifting tomato seedlings he'd grown
as if they were egg shells or Waterford
placing them in rows in my garden
staking them with tree branches
he'd stripped for the purpose
tying them with rags, he'd uniformly cut
to save us some money.

Mary Ann Mannino

∞ Teacher Recognition ∞

Family literacy is one of the educational crusades of the decade. Parents should find time to read with their children, to share books and the love of reading, to pour over the words and pictures, idyllically seated in rocking chairs, next to a crackling fire. My sister Elena and I occasionally tell my mother Camille, or Lizzie, as I will later explain, that because she rarely read to us she was a bad mother. Undaunted by current educational practices, she steadfastly responds, "You turned out all right, didn't you?"

We've often described Lizzie as hyperactive. She has consistently operated at 78 rpms in a 33 1/3 rpm world. I walked home from school each day, only to be greeted by the scent of ammonia and the whining of the vacuum cleaner. It was stressful, but since I was only seven, I thought lunch time was supposed to be that way.

She never focuses upon one activity, but manages to work at many simultaneously: cooking, baking, sewing, cleaning, gardening, shopping, and running the household. Her organizational skills should be packaged and marketed, though I doubt that the average individual has the endurance or stamina to sustain more than a day or two of the "Lizzie Method."

I mentioned that the prepackaged ideal of family literacy did not exist during my childhood, but in all fairness, I must describe Lizzie's brand of teaching and learning. The most important thing that my mother taught me was independence. I have always felt that I was trusted and respected. When the first day of kindergarten arrived and Lizzie asked me if she should walk me to school, I immediately wondered. Why? I know where it is. Imagine my surprise when I saw my classmates clinging to their mothers' skirts.

I learned the magical power of print in Lizzie's kitchen. By second grade I knew how to read recipes and assemble ingredients. (Today it is called having life skills.) The fractions that baffle many of my students were introduced to me in the form of measuring cups and spoons. Later, in third and fourth grades, the pinning and cutting of patterns and the pressing of seams developed my hand-eye coordination and my gift for spatial relations. I deciphered and read mysterious codes of knitting and crochet directions. In short, I came to expect that if I needed to do anything, all I had to do was look it up somewhere, and I'd be able to accomplish my goal.

I've described a very traditional, almost agricultural home life, but that was only one of Lizzie's many facets. When we moved into our new house, she undertook the wallpapering and painting of its rooms while my father was at work. When the monstrous radiators were too ugly to tolerate, she enrolled in the local high school's adult education program. As a result, she built radiator covers and wall units. I know Elena's penchant for power tools dates back to her early childhood and my mother's wood-working projects.

When the sight of my buck teeth were too unbearable for words, Lizzie took a part time job to pay for my orthodontia. When with friends she would have me smile to reveal the rows of metal in my mouth. The part-time employment continued in one form or another, until 1991. This paid for underwriting Elena's orthodontia, two incarnations of wall-to-wall carpeting, baccalaureate degrees for the two of us, a few new and used cars, and a new kitchen. In addition to her regular employment as a laboratory technician, her sewing and design talents were joined to become *Clever, Cuddly, and Camille,* a cottage industry that produced soft sculpture which footed the bill for my wedding reception.

From her given name Camille, we derived chameleon, then lizard, and its refinement, Lizzie. When we coined this name twenty years ago, our mother objected.

"It reminds me of cows. Lizzie, Lizzie Borden, Borden's milk, Elsie the Cow!"

I don't know how our family would fare in psychological tests, but I do know the level quick-witted banter that continues in our home has influenced my sense of humor and enabled me to find amusement in the most pedestrian situations.

As the reigning keeper of the holidays, Lizzie has taught me to cook the Italian foods of my grandmother and great grandmother because, "Somebody has to know how to do it when I'm not here." I predict that decades from now I will find myself making *pasteria di grano* every Easter, even though it's not a food of choice for me or for my sister.

This piece would not be complete without mention of the very special warmth we share, without overt displays of affection through our almost daily interactions and my weekly visits home, where I do my laundry. While there, Lizzie beckons me into the guest room and displays her recent bargains from the Talbot's Outlet, or the most recent curtains and pillows sewn for the upstate house Elena and I share.

Every Sunday evening I return to Queens with recycled ricotta containers filled with home-cooked soups, surplus groceries, clothes ransomed from the dry cleaners, and a feeling of renewal that only laughter, love, and a day on Long Island can bring. There aren't adequate words for that kind of warmth . Except, maybe, "Thank You, Mom!"

Linda Correnti

∞ Aunt Mary's Funeral ∞

Carter Wilson, senior class wit and raconteur, said, "Benevento will turn out to be a town where all the people walk around the central square looking up soulfully at the sky." Everyone laughed but me. It was 1959, my senior year in high school in Washington, D.C. I sat with a group of friends at the local hangout after school. I pictured a bunch of people looking, from my five-foot-eleven vantage point, small and chunky, like my Aunt Amelia and Uncle Freddie, walking around a sunny space with a fountain in the center and their noses in the air. "I don't get it," I said. Everyone laughed again, and Carter, for my benefit, cast an exaggeratedly soulful look toward heaven through the roof of the Hot Shoppe and sighed deeply. I realized that he meant me.

That was what I did these days: I walked around with my head in the clouds, not noticing anything. Much later I could identify the vagueness that charmed my friends as the early symptom of a delayed reaction to my father's death several years earlier and my mother's grief and rage, not to mention my own. At the time, though, I simply thought of myself as preoccupied with higher things. Higher than what? I do not think I answered the question. And Carter was pretending to consider my soulful demeanor a genetic or tribal phenomenon.

Aunt Amelia had been visiting us from New York, and, as I had just finished telling my friends, I had learned the name of the city in Italy from which my grandparents had emigrated. Benevento. It seems so important now to recapture the way in which I was disconnected from any sense of ethnicity or family and of what ethnicity and, especially, family meant to my place in the world. The only ethnic reality present to me growing up in the 40's and 50's in Washington, D.C., was the gulf between black and white, which I did not yet notice.

Benevento. There was power in that word. It made me want to know more about my long dead grandfather, and grandmother, who lived upstairs from Aunt Amelia and Uncle Freddie with her two unmarried children. I knew so little about customs and culture that I made no connection between her unfailingly somber clothes and my grandfather's death, which had taken place when my father was only fourteen. I didn't recognize the fact that my grandmother's appearance actually subverted the stereotype of the Italian widow. In her black shawl, long black dress, black cotton stockings and black lumpy shoes, she stood five feet eleven inches, unlike any of her six children, none of whom were particularly tall. She was a big strong woman who laughed at everything, even though her view of the world was essentially gloomy.

My mother kept me away from all these relatives, her Catholic in-laws with Brooklyn accents. Her own background was middle class German Protestant, and she had contempt for her in-laws. A tense, angry person, she could not tolerate the effusive familiarity of her husband's family, the ease with which they drew people into their circle, including me — away from her. I was therefore completely unfamiliar with the culture of lower middle-class Italian American Catholic family life. I rarely saw my aunts and uncles and cousins, but when I did, I adored them. Their home, their family circle, was a place to relax into warm familiarity.

When my Aunt Mary died, in 1986, I had not seen or spoken with any of my family on my father's side for more than two and a half years. Aunt Mary was the oldest daughter in the family of six children, the oldest girl and the only one to remain unmarried. She lived with her mother and bachelor brother. Aunt Mary was a victim of a hit-and-run driver on her way home from the Senior Center in Queens and died five months later. I had always thought of her as a victim, the lonely spinster, low on the family totem pole. Her death seemed horribly appropriate. It began with not having the privilege of leaving home and getting married and ended with her lying bloody by the side of the road.

When my mother called to tell me what had happened, I expressed dismay and sadness, but managed to ask a couple of questions. "Where is the wake? When is the funeral service? When will she be buried?"

It seems as if every Catholic novel or memoir I have ever read talks about the heavy scent of funeral flowers, and now, at my first wake, I knew why. I have Catholic friends who hate cut flowers, period, because of that sole association. On either side of the coffin stood a huge floral arrangement, including two immense crosses made of gladioli, as straight and stiff as the corpse. There were anthurium, those unnatural looking tropical flowers, with one gaping reddish leathery petal encircling the yellow swollen pistil like something out of a sexual nightmare. Large ribbons, placed at the bottom of each display, had messages inscribed on them on a strip of golden ribbon: "Beloved Neighbor," "Beloved Sister." Flowers I normally like, like roses and carnations, were part of these arrangements also, but all of them looked militarily rigid and artificial.

No one was paying much attention to the star attraction, possibly because the wake had been ongoing for three days. When we first came in, Aunt Amelia sobbed noisily for a few seconds, kneeling at the side of the casket, her head resting on the edge very close to Aunt Mary's clasped hands, but then she got up quite briskly and started chatting with neighbors. Cousin Barbara became preoccupied with the size of the crowd in the funeral home. Three days earlier, every room had been occupied with a dead body; today there was only one other corpse, and it, too, would be buried today. My first wake. My first corpse. My own Aunt Mary dead in her coffin. I looked carefully at Aunt Mary in her royal blue polyester taffeta dress, her dyed carrot red hair, her bright red fingernails with crystal rosary beads draped gracefully through her fingers. Pinned on the satin lining of the coffin was a rosary of real roses chained together like a child's daisy chain, the only pretty thing in the room.

It took me some time to figure out why Aunt Mary looked so unlike Aunt Mary. They had her chin wrong. Aunt Mary had been old for quite a while, and jowly; her live face was pretty much straight from her mouth to her breastbone. Now she had the jaw line of a twenty-year-old, her chin forming a too-perfect right angle with her neck. Her mouth was also wrong. In life, she had an Italian mouth, like my grandmother, with a long upper jaw, broad and thin-lipped and turned down at the corners, but capable of a curled smile of total delight. The morticians made her mouth an even line, turned up the corners in a half smile of sweet repose.

"Sin is measured, not by what one does," explained the priest in his eulogy at Aunt Mary's funeral, "but by the dignity of the person affronted." This was by way of illuminating a problem he had just laid before us, the apparent lack of mercy on the part of God in consigning humankind to pain and suffering for the crime of eating a piece of forbidden fruit.

I had learned the night before, from Cousin Rose, after everyone else had gone to bed, that Aunt Mary at the time of her death was receiving $386 a month from the Social Security Administration and another $40 a month from the International Ladies Garment Workers Union, of which she had been a member for almost sixty years. Her rent was $300 a month. That left $126 a month, in the Borough of Queens, New York, in 1986, for everything else. The god of the funeral sermon could not be expected to show mercy toward Aunt Mary's sins.

After the funeral, our limousine followed the hearse along the dirty residential streets of Queens, bumping through potholes and detouring around construction sites. The houses, remembered from the best times of my childhood, are narrow, usually two houses in brick or stucco, joined together, their small back yards divided from each other by steel wire fences. The driveways separated them from the next attached houses on either side.

The backyards of the houses remembered from my childhood visits to Queens were tiny and miraculous, with fig trees and flowers, vegetable plants weighted to the ground with tomatoes, peppers, eggplant, carrots, and peas. There was an extraordinary sense of lushness, ripeness, in these little squares of garden. And such contradictions—the sections that weren't dripping with life were cemented over.

The hearse stopped in front of 109-55-110th Street, Richmond Hill, Queens; our limousine stopped behind it. It was Aunt Mary's house. Where did this custom originate —a last stop in front of the last house she lived in? This street was deserted; the neighbors hadn't returned from church yet. Surely in the old country, in the hill town outside of Benevento, the churchgoers would all have been part of one procession behind a cart bearing the flower-covered coffin, drawn by horses.

We sat there for a minute or two, looking at the house in which Aunt Mary had lived the last part of her life. The dwelling from which she had set out each morning for the Senior Citizens Center, or in summer, for the subway out to Rockaway Beach. Aunt Amelia said, "Be sure to notice where we go now, as we drive to the cemetery —I want to show you something. Just be careful to notice distances."

So I kept looking out the window, at block after block of semidetached houses, stucco, fake brick, stucco, frame, fake brick. The neighborhood had changed, as two generations of Italian-Americans moved out toward Long Island, and then, like my Aunt Amelia and Uncle Freddie, to further parts, ahead of the blacks and Puerto Ricans leaving the inner city. In my childhood, Italian was the language of Lefferts Boulevard, the principal street of the neighborhood, where Uncle Freddie had his butcher shop. Now English and Spanish are spoken there.

I had no sense of direction in Queens, but our limousine had made a number of turns in the mile and a half or so since stopping at Aunt Mary's house. Aunt Amelia said, "See over there, that building next to the church?" A low cinderblock structure. "That is the Senior Center. She went there, walked there every day—almost two miles! Everyone in the whole neighborhood knew her. Children would talk to her as she went by their yards. A couple of the old people said that they could set their clocks by her. Every day, she went that way at the same time—that's why she was so healthy and could do so much, until her accident. She went into the city all the time to go to the ballet or to see a show. She'd get all dressed up and go, sometimes with a friend, but sometimes just by herself. She was interested in everything!"

My grandfather died in 1925 and was buried in one of the first cemeteries for Italians in this country, in Forest Hills. "Many of the first wave of immigrants are buried here," said Uncle Harry. Some of the monuments were massive pieces of architecture . Many had finely chiseled letters that said "Riposa in pace."

Still, there it was, the family plot. Two plain granite slabs, partially covered by the fake-grass-covered tarpaulins which hid the earth and digging from our eyes. But I could see a version of our family name decreed to us on some document by some immigration official.

"Leviero," it said in fine Roman capitals.

Aunt Mary is gone. I never allowed her to be important to me when she was alive. When I was little, she embarrassed me, with the clashing reds of her hair and nails, her bright garish clothes, her many necklaces and bracelets. She smiled that wide smile at me and came too close. Now I've discovered my kinship with her. I must still worry about my hard heart, but only for myself. Aunt Mary didn't need me, with her $380 a month, living alone, with no one but the neighborhood to love her. She had fun, every day, as regular as clockwork, and knew she was appreciated by others.

A fantasy began in 1959 with the pretty sound of "Benevento." I pictured the moving luggage belt at the Rome airport and many secret rehearsals with a phrasebook. I pictured trains and buses and helpful people. But it is still the same dream that started then, of getting there, arriving there, and then, via the telephone book or the records of some church, finding them. The genealogical details are necessarily fuzzy, but there is a door opening and a lighted room and a small crowd of people who welcome me and love me—and I, them—only because we are related.

Toni H. Oliviero

∞ That's the Way it Was ∞

In Sicily, grandpa's family was quite affluent and as a result when he departed for the United States he carried with him cash and jewels. It was a sufficient resource to get him started in the new world, in Brooklyn.

Grandpa invested in several apartment buildings, which he leased, and also in a store which sold produce. He was not a very good businessman. Selling produce was not a money maker and to make matters worse, the local Mafia told grandpa that he could no longer buy his produce from the local market. He would have to buy from their supplier at a considerably higher price.

Undaunted, grandpa decided to purchase his produce across the Hudson River in New Jersey. One day, when my father's younger brother drove his truck to pick up the produce, the family received a telephone call from the State Police. The truck had been stopped, the produce strewn all over the road, and dad's brother had been beaten and was in the hospital. Nothing life threatening, but scary. Dad and grandpa were ready to do battle with the "mob" but cooler and wiser heads prevailed.

The advice for grandpa was that he should meet with the local godfather, who happened to have emigrated from the same town in Sicily as grandpa – Corleone. After the meeting and since blood is thicker than water, grandpa was allowed to make his purchases in New Jersey, with the godfather's approval, of course.

When my father was a teenager in Brooklyn during the prohibition years, he obtained a chauffeur's license because he was offered a job driving for a local businessman. His father, my grandfather, queried him one day, concerning his job. Dad replied that his job was simple. All he had to do was to drive a man around to different business establishments: stores, restaurants, laundries, etc. While Dad waited in the car, the man would enter the place of business carrying a bag. After a few minutes the man would get back in the car with the bag and direct Dad to the next location.

It didn't take long for grandpa to figure out what the "bag man" was doing and for whom he was working. He urged dad to quit his job and to "play it safe." He moved his family to the Bronx.

But we were really a typical Italian immigrant family in the Bronx. All of grandpa's siblings, uncles, aunts, and cousins settled within walking distance, a few living next door to one another, three houses in a row. It felt great growing up in my neighborhood. I would walk into any of the houses as if they were my own and sample the delicious Old World cooking. We were always welcome in each other's homes and all the children seemed to belong to any household they happened to wander into.

The warmth, love, security of this familial existence has remained with me through the years, and the one thing I miss most is the loss of that family closeness. We all grew up and went our separate ways. The old ones have passed on as one of my cousins remarked recently, "The only time we see each other is at weddings, a special family celebration, or at a funeral." Sad, but true. The passing of an era – it passed with the older generation: the end of a way of life. Have we become too *American*?

Lou Gennaro

∞ The Old Gang ∞

We were a bunch of Italian American teenage guys sitting on the steps of the Rochester Welding Works' at the corner of Orchard Street and Riley Place every evening, weather permitting. Today, we refer to ourselves as "The Old Gang." Original members included Maurice Tette, Nick Morante, Pat DeCillis, Mariano Bianchi, Angelo Tantalo, Mike Lamendola, Joe Palumbo, John and Frank Andolina, Eddie Maruggi, Larry Vaccarelli, and Joe Micciche. We came from the Lyell Avenue, Broad Street, Lime Street, Riley Place, Orchard Street, Jay Street neighborhood. We all attended #17 Eli Whitney Elementary School and James Madison High School in Rochester, New York.

Most of our parents came to this country from Italy's poor south and Sicily during the early 1900's while others came in the 1920's. They were hard working people; construction workers, laborers, railroad builders, shoe factory employees, and clothing factory workers, trying to support their families in a new environment.

The Welding Works' steps is where we learned about the birds and the bees from the older guys. On the grass in front of this building is where we played mumbley peg, horses, and hot box. Across Orchard Street, in the A.C. Delco cinder- filled parking lot, we played soft ball, sometimes a triple-header. One softball taped and/or stitched together several times, would last us all summer. The baseball bats were cracked but a nail here or a screw there, plus friction tape, would hold the bats together. I don't recall any of our group ever owning a new baseball mitt.

We competed in sports against other teens in adjoining neighborhoods, in baseball and football. We had our own sports arena, a building on Riley Place where we constructed a bowling alley, a basketball court, and a boxing ring. Outdoors of the arena we pitched horseshoes. This was my neighborhood in the late 30's and early 40's before World War II separated us.

During the War, a few quit school to support their families. Most of the others went into military service. After the War we married, some went off to college to take advantage of the G I Bill, while others went to work in clothing factories, chemical industries, Eastman Kodak, the fuel oil business and General Motors. These changes in our lives did not diminish our close relationship.

In the late 40's, after the War had ended, we continued to meet annually at Monroe County parks; we played softball, horseshoes, and bocci, stuffed ourselves with spaghetti and meatballs, and drank wine and beer. Our physical energy has lessened over the years so instead of playing softball or even playing bocci, today, some fifty-five years later, we have breakfast or lunch together every two months.

When we meet we still tell "remember when" stories, brag about various things we did or about the times we skipped school to go to a burlesque show, attended football games at Edgerton Park, or the occasions when some of us drove to Batavia, to visit "ladies of the game" in Batavia's "Red Light" district.

We still tend to use the "nick names" we used many years ago when we refer to one another, names like; "Mudd," "Mowdy," "Weasel," "Cigars," "JP," "Stretch," "Kekale," "Mitch," "Butch," and "Popman." A few members of the "Old Gang" have passed on but our collective spirit and friendship have not changed.

Nick Morante

∞ Multi-Ethnic Love and Respect ∞

As I write this narrative on Wednesday, the 27th of November 2002, I have a very heavy heart, because my daughter Therese's funeral took place yesterday. She had been mentally ill for thirty years. Her life ended suddenly by her own hand five days ago while a patient in a mental health unit of a local hospital. It is not about her that I write, however. It is in regard to what I believed to be solely an Italian or an Italian American expression of love and respect by neighbors and friends. What an incorrect assumption it was.

During the week of Therese's wake our family was overwhelmed by the response of our neighbors and close friends. To help us cope with the sadness and shock of our loss they supplied our home with food and visits. Last Saturday, Deanne and Gary Delehanty drove over to our house and delivered a large pan of baked ziti, a salad, a loaf of French bread, and a panetone. They had dinner with us that evening to be with us in our time of need.

Monday, Rosemarie and Tony Toscano brought a large tray of finger sandwiches of tuna, ham, turkey, and egg salad, and also home baked cookies. Tony returned this morning, which is Thankgiving Day, with a home baked pumpkin pie and a magnum of Tony's homemade white wine.

Sylvia Driscoll who lives across the street baked a huge chocolate cake and delivered it Monday night. She walked over to our home in the dark, even though she is sight impaired. Also on that same day, Jane and Joe Mileo came to visit and brought a large aluminum pan of a warm broccoli casserole, fresh grapes, a loaf of olive bread, and a magnum of Pinot Grigio wine. Tuesday, Marv and Sora Sachs delivered an apple-nut bundt cake that Sora had baked.

At the funeral parlor on Tuesday, Rosemary and Vinnie Fazio brought a dish of homemade Italian style cookies. And on Wednesday morning Anne Camhi and her sister Esther Granite phoned to say that they would like to deliver dinner to our home on a day of our choice. And would we like chicken or oriental food?

I do not believe this wonderful expression of caring by our friends and neighbors was unique to us. I believe it is replicated in various degrees over and over in every community regardless of the nationality or ethnicity.

This gesture on the part of some very special people helped ease our pain during this difficult period. To them my family is grateful.

Edward Albert Maruggi

Games and Humor

Grandma Yogi

∞ Grandma Yogi ∞

Yogi-isms have become as much a part of the fabric of our American culture as hot dogs. Invoking the comic imagery of the quotations of the beloved malapropist Yogi Berra is a pastime unto itself with quotations such as, "Nobody goes there anymore because it's too crowded," and, "When you come to the fork in the road, take it."

I don't know the origin and history of malapropism of the English language. Is it endemic only to those who grew up in Italian-speaking households but learned English later in life? I ask this because my grandmother Teresa Maruggi shared with Yogi the same Italian heritage, and the same way with words. Whenever I hear Yogi speak I think of my grandmother, and, "It's like deja vu all over again."

Still Grandma's expressions were uniquely her own. More often than not you can easily deduce Yogi's intent, but with Grandma, it's a different story. Can you guess these key words from the lines below? (Imagine a heavy Italian accent for the voice of grandma).

Jeep
Me: "Grandma, how did you travel to Florida for
    your vacation?"
Grandma: "I went by Jeep."
Translation: Jet

Five-by-five
Grandma: "Turn on the five-by-five so I can listen to
        some music."
Translation: Hi-fi (stereo system)

Tuxedo

Me: "Grandma, why did they wait so long to bury your
friend who passed away?"
Grandma: "Because they had to perform a tuxedo."
Translation: Autopsy

Throw-Up Rug

Grandma: "Don't forget to put down the throw-up rug
after you wash the floor."
Translation: "Throw rug"

Socialite

Grandma: "I can't see the numbers on the TV dial, go
get me a socialite."
Translation: Searchlight (flashlight)

Gangrenes

Grandma: "It's cold outside, so put on your gangrenes."
Translation: Dungarees (jeans)

Torpedo

Me: "I stopped by to see you in the hospital today but
you weren't in your room."
Grandma: "They took me downstairs to the lab for
some torpedo."
Translation: Therapy

Cadillacs and Gonorrhea

Me: "Grandma, I heard you went to the opthamologist
yesterday, how are your eyes?"
Grandma: " They're fine. The doctor said I don't have
cadillacs or gonorrhea."
Translation: Cataracts or glaucoma

Two Toes
If an automobile or a piece of furniture was two different colors. It was "Two Toes."
Translation: Two tone

Liquid Store
Grandma: "Edward, when you go to the liquid store, buy me a case of red Martini & Rossi wine."
Translation: Liquor Store

And last but not least, Grandma's question to my sister when she was a teenager and nearing puberty.

"Susan, did you begin to demonstrate yet?"

Edward P. Maruggi

∞ Oh! Brother ∞

My mother and father had great respect for the clergy. While they did not agree with everything that priests said, they respected the role that priests had. As for Brothers, they had never heard of one. Therefore, when my widowed mother heard from me at twenty-one years of age that I was going into a teaching order of Brothers, the De La Salle Christian Brothers, she was dumbfounded. Once and only once did she state her resentment to this plan for my vocational future. She said that she could understand a priest giving up having a family – a wife and children – but becoming a Brother? For What? You can't say Mass, do baptisms, hear confessions, or do other priestly duties.

As a Brother, a few years later when I came home for a short visit, she and I went off to an early morning weekday

Mass at the parish church. As we walked down the main aisle before Mass, she stopped at a few pews to greet some of her friends and said to them, *"Quest e il mio figlio Vincenzo, la monica."*

During mass, I couldn't concentrate because I was distracted by what my mother had said. Although I had failed Italian in high school with a final grade of forty-eight percent, I remembered that masculine nouns ended in "o" or "i" and feminine in "a" or "e" depending if they were singular or plural. Did the Italian language have a word for monk? If it did, why wasn't it equivalent to the English noun, *sisters*? When we started to walk home after Mass, I asked my mother if she had used the wrong word for monk. My question to her was,

"Shouldn't you have said *il monico* instead of *la monica*?

Didn't you call me a nun instead of a monk?"I said. She looked straight ahead and answered with a little annoyance and resignation in her voice,

"What's the difference! You can't have children."

Vincent Ortolani

∞ Scopa ∞

From the look on my brother's face, I couldn't tell whether he had settore or not. This was anxiety provoking. If he had settore I would not throw down my three of hearts. If he didn't have it, then I would: well, I think I will. Maybe I'd be better off throwing the six of hearts. But then, Nanna could, sometimes, make a Settanta-Settore with sixes, so maybe I should hang on to the six a little longer.

Hmmmmmm. Well!

"Scopa!" My cousin triumphantly let the queen of diamonds fall, sweeping away (as the word *Scopa* in

Italian means) the five of hearts, the two of spades, and the ace of diamonds. He gleefully added the trick to his growing pile of winnings. Not only was it a *Scopa!* – worth a point in itself, but it was also a four card catch and two diamonds, at that.

Tom, my brother had an alarmed look on his face.

"I knew it," I thought to myself, "he's got the Settore and he's going to throw it down."

Christie, my other cousin, had the next play. Forlornly, she dropped the seven of hearts on the table. "Scopa!" – shouted Tom, diving forward to play the seven of diamonds – the coveted Settore – over Christie's card.

"Oh!" The rest of us groaned. He'd gained two sure points with the play and now had a chance to get a complete set of four – seven cards, the most valuable cards in the game.

Soon enough, the game was finished and it was time to add up the scores. We always consulted our Nanna or mothers about this. It was not difficult to do some of the scoring ourselves. "Number of cards" was easy enough, with one point going to the player who had amassed the most cards. "Most diamonds" was also easy; each player merely counted the diamond-suit cards they had won. The Scopa-plays were pretty simple. I was always the one who had trouble keeping track because I would look at and rearrange my cards while the game was still going on, getting the Scopa – plays mixed up among the rest of my pile.

But the most difficult cards to figure out were the Settanta-Settores. Nanna was the one who *really* knew which ones counted, and as far as I can tell, she still may be chuckling over it from her portal in heaven. The ideal Settanta-Settore is to possess all four of the seven-cards (seven-of-hearts, diamonds, spades, and clubs) – in one's winning hand at the end of the game. The most valuable of the four is the seven-of-diamonds, which had a name of its own, "Settore." If you had that card, you received a point for just having it by itself. Nanna would take all the cards and go through them to find the sevens. She'd lay them out like a four square. If you didn't have all four sevens, then she would start substituting with sixes or, sometimes, fives. If you had the Settore and the seven of hearts that, somehow, was more valuable than having the Settore and the seven of spades or clubs. But, if you had the Settore plus the seven of spades and the seven of clubs, she would let you put in the six of hearts or even the five of hearts and say, "Now that's a Settanta-Settore!" Nanna's word was <u>final</u>. I was always mystified on how she justified that decision.

We would play Scopa for hours. Scopa-plays and winnings of diamond-cards were small triumphs, but we lived to find out who would be the lucky one to be dealt the settore or other sevens. The game always began with a shuffle through the deck of cards to get rid of all the eights, nines, and tens. Italian card games are usually played with a deck of forty cards, with the Jacks, Queens, and Kings counted in Scopa for eight, nine, and ten, respectively. At Nanna's house the cards were always ready for other card games as well.

As we grew older we would, sometimes, play in teams or partners. This would be confusing as well as stimulating. My mother was a proponent of the team concept. She had all sorts of tactics on how partners could increase their combined winnings. "If you had the Settore, scratch behind your ear," she'd suggest. This ploy worked for awhile until I inadvertently scratched behind my ear just because it was itching. Once, when my cousin Cammie and I were partners I actually believed that I had the Settore, and let a six fall. An ace was already on the table, and before I realized it, my other cousin had captured both the six and the ace with the real Settore. Cammie was steamed. My sorry excuse didn't count for much. As a result, we developed a whole set of "signals" – tapping one's nose, winking, crossing one's legs a certain way, etc.

Over the years, the interest in Scopa waned to be replaced by Hearts, Rummy, and Poker. Three years ago, while on a trip to Italy, I found a playing deck of cards while browsing in a little shop in a northern city. Its cards had beautiful colored figures in all four suits; cups, coins, swords, and batons. It also had only forty cards. It was a true Italian deck. Slowly, my memory returned to the sounds of childlike voices crying "Scopa, Scopa." I could visualize the group of us seated around the table in Nanna's living room, intent on our game. I purchased the deck and learned from the shop's proprietor that there are many styles of card decks in Italy, reflecting different regions and cities. I began to imagine that perhaps a century ago, Nanna could have played with a deck like this in Calabria where she lived as a young girl.

As I write this, my one-year old daughter, Elsa Maddalena, plays contentedly at my feet. Her older cousins, my brother's children, are beginning to learn card games like *Go Fish!* and *Concentration*. I think the next time we all get together, I will pull out the deck I bought in Italy, and show the pretty figures and sayings on the cards and we can start learning the sequences and how to match the suits. And when the children are a little older, we can all learn how to play Scopa again. I must be sure to send a spirit-message to Nanna – so I can figure out how she counted the cards and always ended up with Settanta-Settore.

Francesca Taylor

∞ Mrs. Seminario ∞

Our family were renters during the mid nineteen twenties. The landlord was Mr. Arnone. He and his family were temporarily hosting their relatives, the Seminario family, from Peoria, Illinois who were relocating to Rochester, New York. Within a few weeks the newcomers were able to find housing within our neighborhood and soon the Seminario, Arnone, and Cappiello children became close friends. Through the Arnones, we heard that the Seminario family included two Hollywood movie actors – namely Tom Tyler and his sister, Olive Borden. Despite skepticism and disbelief on the part of some residents in the neighborhood concerning the Seminario-Hollywood connection, the closeness of our relationship with Arnones and Seminarios left no doubt concerning the authenticity.

The era of cowboy silent movies flourished during this period with the names of Tom Mix, and Hoot Gibson, among others, in almost every child's vocabulary. On the other hand, adults more prominently recognized the name of Olive Borden. My brother Dave and I recall going to the Astor Theater to see cowboy movies on Saturday afternoons along with Tony and Willie Seminario and their cousins, Richard and Joe Arnone. When Tom Tyler's movies were featured we would sit in the front row and view two and sometimes three showings of the same movie, while munching a supper of homemade sandwiches. Often, during suspenseful intervals, we would root for our hero. Later, during the week, we would spend time reliving and discussing the events we had seen on the screen.

I remember the time Mrs. Seminario was in the movie theater and sitting directly behind me as we watched her son Tom Tyler on the silver screen. During a very exciting moment the "bad guy," was up to no good, cowardly sneaking up to assault Tom. Suddenly, and instinctively Mrs. Seminario yelled loudly in her Sicilian dialect, "Feegyoo Mio! Doona cura ah keedoo sonama bee cho!" (My son! Look out for that S. O. B.) Needless to say, I have remembered that outburst to this very day.

Joseph Cappiello

∞ Tombola ∞

Tombola, a family game similar to Bingo was played on wintry evenings, on the eve of a feast, or during the Christmas Novena, after the evening church service. Young and old played it, often with neighboring families. As in Bingo, each player buys a card or two for a small coin, one or two soldi (cents).

Each card had fifteen scrambled numbers on it, the numerical range being from one to ninety. The fifteen numbers were laid out five across and three rows down. We used ceci beans to fill in the numbers, if called. Filling in two numbers was an ambo, three terno, four, quaterna, five cinquina, and filling in all fifteen numbers was tombola. The caller would draw the numbers; one to ninety stamped on little wooden blocks, from a bag. The caller played with six cards, which included all ninety numbers.

When everyone had a card or cards, and had paid for them, the players decided what the various prizes would be: tombola was the highest. It was now time for the game to begin. As the caller shook the bag, the little blocks were drawn out one at a time with the caller giving each number a nickname. For example: 1 is Italy (Italia una), referring to the unification of Italy), married couple, 2; a kitten, 3; pig's feet, 4; Saint Nicholas, 6 (Saint Nicholas' day is December 6th); Maria, 8 (the Immaculate Conception is on December 8th); girl's legs, 11; a dozen, 12; Lucia, 13 (Saint Lucy's day is December 13th); Christmas, 25; Saint Stephen, 26; the corpse that does not speak (*il morto che non parla*), 31; the Lord's age, 33; the corpse that speaks (*il morto che parla*), 47; revolution, 48, (the year of Italy's revolution); *mezzo quintale*, 50, etc. The caller had free reign to name each number that he or she wished. The funny ones brought snickers and laughter from participants.

Because the number of players was not limited, it was not unusual to have ten to twelve participating in the game, with several others watching. As a result, the chatter was continuous and noise level high as shouts of joy accompanied each winner. The person who was the first to cover his or her card with all fifteen numbers would yell "TOMBOLA" (instead of "Bingo") because the person who made tombola not only won the largest prize, but also the right to be the caller for the next game.

When the play ended fruit, nuts, and dessert were brought to the table, and when mother told her children to say *grazie e buona notte* (thank you and good night) to the host they went home *felici e contenti* (happy and contented). Those who played tombola in family circles on wintry evenings will, forever, cherish the memory.

Today, this game is no longer popular.

Vittorio Re

∞ What Chicken? ∞

My grandfather was a simple man: simple tastes and simple pleasures, but not simpleminded. Although he had barely attended grade school, he read the newspaper daily, and listened each afternoon to the stock market report broadcast over the radio. And though his antics often filled his children with discomfort, he was able to disengage himself from almost any hopeless situation with quick thinking and, yes, simple logic. "What red light, officer? I never saw it change."

At my grandfather's seventieth birthday gathering, he announced to the family that he intended to take a trip back to his *paese,* a small town in Umbria called Portaria, where he had left his widowed mother and brother fifty years earlier. He had always been an industrious man. He lived in Germany at the age of fifteen to work in the steel mills of Essen, and sailed to America at twenty-two years of age. He owned a car way before most of his *compari,* and moved his family from Harlem to the Bronx to Brooklyn. He even saved enough money to purchase land in upstate New York. The land there was much like that of Italy, but he never spoke of returning to his birthplace; he and his Calabrian wife Francesca had made America their home.

Now he was going back to visit his brother and the family that balanced out the Medori family on the other side of the Atlantic Ocean. The impending trip became, as all things did, an undertaking for the entire family. My uncle bought him stylish luggage. My aunts purchased new apparel, from underwear to suits. My mother helped him secure a passport, and make travel arrangements for purchasing flight insurance. She sewed my grandmother a new navy blue linen dress.

The paparazzi were there, everywhere, the day of his

departure. Shutters snapped as Nonno posed in front of a flower bed, his suitcase in one hand, Nonna with her bonnet and gloves in the other. They were elegant – successful landowners, family patriarchs. But something was wrong with this picture. Nonna was not going with him. She said she had everything she needed right here in America and had no desire to revisit her birthplace. She was petrified of flying, we all suspected. And so the photos were staged, for some odd reason, as if the stately couple were taking off together when, in fact, Nonno was going back the same way he had come – alone.

The entourage of family members followed him to the airport in caravan fashion. They saw him board, laden with gifts for his Italian family. They asked the passenger sitting next to him to please look after him, he was elderly and had never been in an airplane. They snapped more photos and documented everything.

Postcards began arriving two weeks later. They were all addressed to my grandmother and formally signed, *Tuo sposato Adolfo Medori*, as though she might have forgotten who he was. But the postcards had not been written by my grandfather and were, instead, written by his nephew – something that puzzled us all.

On a hot afternoon in August the paparazzi were all back at Idlewild Airport to welcome Nonno home from his journey, gather him and his belongings up, and whisk him away where he would once again be under the safety net of the family. How they had endured his absence now floored them. Their anticipation of his arrival was almost uncontainable.

"There he is!" We shouted from the observatory deck as he began to descend the steps of the Alitalia aircraft.

"Who?" the woman standing alongside me eagerly asked, expecting maybe Sofia Loren, Marcello Mastroianni, or the Beatles. "Who is it?" she persisted.

139 /Games and Humor

"My grandfather," I said, pulling the rug of excitement out from under her.

From the second floor glass wall, we watched Nonno going through the customs line below. He seemed to be experiencing difficulty with the customs official who was searching through his belongings. The young man shook a finger at Nonno prohibiting him to continue past the customs area. He called a co-worker over to discuss the problem. With a look of innocence, Nonno cast both hands in the air in a display of exasperation and despair. What illegal act could he have committed? This was a man whose loyalty to America was absolute. He was known to have left a sick bed to cast a ballot on Election Day. Our hearts went out to him. But our sympathy soured when two stewardesses walked past us, laughing about the old man who had a chicken in his suitcase.

"Dead or alive?" my mother asked, knowing that her father was capable of almost anything.

My embarrassed aunts nearly swooned. My uncles murmured Italian curses. Was there no end to the lengths that their father would go to humiliate them? On the other hand, my cousins and I found the situation most amusing. When Nonno finally exited the customs area, his children escorted him to the parking lot. They barely spoke to him. He settled his overweight body into the Chevy Bel Air with difficulty, heaved a sigh of relief, and said that it was good to be home.

With a voice void of apologies he began to explain about the chicken. Nonno's relatives had celebrated his visit with the constant preparation of rich foods like wild pheasant, turkey, and rabbit stew. He, in turn, suffered an attack of gout so severe that he remained bedridden for two weeks unable even to sign his name. In gratitude for the care he received from those who had unknowingly caused his illness, Nonno left them all of his new clothes, but he had not returned with an empty suitcase.

Later, in the comfort of his home, he opened the suitcase and with gleeful satisfaction revealed the bounty he had escaped with. First to emerge from the baggage was a small fig tree, then a cake, then garlic bulbs to be transplanted in his garden. Also removed were chestnuts, a quantity of rooted olive branches, and, of course, the chicken roasted to perfection on an open pit and carefully wrapped in grape leaves for protection.

"Derra was a leg ova homa mada prosciutto, but dose *mascalzoni* at the Rome airport taka dat away from me. Dey say itsa no legal, but dey know a gooda ting when dey see it." He said, begrudgingly conceding to defeat.

"But, Nonno, how did you ever get through U. S. Customs with all this stuff?" I asked, knowing that plants were definitely forbidden.

"I tell 'em I hava longa trip to go home. I tol 'em I gottta no family, no food, only dis stuff. I'm alone inna disa world."

"And they believed you?"

"Ma sura, Foista, I check derra nametags and I maka sura dat no customs person isa Italian."

Marisa Labozzetta

∞ Language of the Old Italo-Americano ∞

Since many immigrants came from agricultural areas in Southern Italy, their knowledge of industrial terms was minimal; consequently, many words were phonetically Italianized. Therefore, job was *jobba*; an assembly line was a *lyna*; a car was a *carro* similar to the word for Italian wagon, or vehicle and a streetcar was a *carro elettrico*. The foreman on a job was a *caporale* because he acted like an army corporal. A supervisor was *bosso*. Anyone in command was *bosso, bigga bosso* if really the top man. Depending on his character the boss was also a *son a 'magogna* (son of a gun) or a *son a'ma bicce* (S.O.B.)

At times the boss might be *roffo* or a *naysa* man. His paycheck was in an *enveloppa* (envelope). If a man was a *briccalaya* (bricklayer) he worked with *a genga* (gang) making *a ruffe* (roof) or *a basementi* (basement). On the job it was necessary to have *inchunz* (insurance) because if on the job you make a *mistecca* (mistake), the *bille* (bills) would not to be paid.

Merica (America) is a free *kon-tree* (country). Giorgio Washingtonne was wella known becausa when you apply for citizenship the first question was an still isa, "Who was the first President of the United States?" Giorgio Washingtonne, *ma shoos* (for sure).

Mericani lika eyesa scrima, an dey also lika foota bolla. Oh yes dey lika to bolla, too. If you are lezy an start monkee bisinissi, oncolo Sem will give you plenty of trobbolee. Lissen to me, younghe man: marry nice Italian girl, maka good children and when you are old, you can sit on the front porcio and watch your yarda. Shoo, gud bay and Gad bless.

Vittorio Re

∞ Oops! ∞

My husband, Edward, and I were fortunate to have lived in Italy for an academic year. He was the recipient of a Rotary Foundation Fellowship in 1980/81. The award was called "Teacher of the Handicapped Award," because of his work with college level deaf students at Rochester Institute of Technology. The purpose of the award was three-fold; to conduct research at a grade school in Milan, to study at the Catholic University of the Sacred Heart, and to be a goodwill ambassador for the United States. It was a great opportunity for us to live for several months in the country of his parent's origin.

During the first two months of our stay, we lived with an Italian family in Florence where he was taking a two-month long Italian language course. The academic week was such that it provided us with an opportunity to travel on weekends to visit some of Italy's ancient and most scenic tourist attractions.

One beautiful sun drenched Saturday in late September, we decided to visit the hilltop town of Volterra, known for its scenic view of the valley below as well as its highly recommended archeological museum. We found the museum in a large garden filled with stone relics of ancient buildings. At the rear of the garden stood a large three-story building that appeared to be an old castle. After exploring the garden's grounds we decided that the castle must be an internal extension of the museum. Undeterred that there was no entrance from the garden, we walked around the building and found a high, arched, thick wooden door at the rear of the structure. Along the path leading up to the door we noticed several signs that read *Vietato!*

Non di Entrare! meaning, 'forbidden' and 'do not enter.'

We knew what the signs meant, but were unsure if it applied to us. I was hesitant but my husband forged ahead. A man stood very erect at the castle's door and Edward walked up to him. He immediately asked what we wanted. Edward responded in his very best Italian that we wished to gain entrance to the building. He inquired as to whether we had seen the signs. We said "Si, Si." He shook his head and asked if we were Americans. Again we replied "Si." This time he shook his head vigorously, and peered at us digustedly. "You Americans are all alike," he said, shooing us away with a hand movement.

By this time he was joined by a gentleman in uniform who gave us a stern, military, look. Unsure of what we had done wrong, and disappointed that we had failed in our mission to tour the inside of the castle, we left as instructed.

Monday morning after his language class had ended, my husband approached the instructor, who had told him earlier in the semester that she resided in Volterra. When she learned of our interest in attempting to gain entrance into the Volterra castle, her astonishment turned to laughter when she told him that fifty of Italy's most dangerous terrorists of the Red Brigade were imprisoned there.

Carolyn B. Maruggi

∞ Sopra e Sotto ∞

While growing up in an Italian American family, I observed Friday night card games. The favorite game was called *Sopra e Sotto*, literally meaning, "Boss and Under-boss." It was played in a type of seven card, open-face poker format. No money changed hands in this game, only alcoholic drinks. It was played, primarily, by the same group of Italian American males: my father, grandfather, uncles, and a couple of close friends and other relatives.

This card game was played almost every week and rotated from house to house. When playing at our house, the six to eight players sat around a table in our basement with a drinking glass for each participant. The size of the glass depended on the beverage being served, wine or beer. The empty glasses were placed in the center of the table, then the dealer dealt the cards to the individual players. A player could not drop out of the game as one would be allowed to do in poker. At the end of each deal the player with the highest poker hand and the one with the lowest poker hand were the key players in the next phase of the game.

The glasses were filled with, say, wine. The player with the highest hand was the "Boss." The player with the lowest hand became the "Underboss." The Boss had control over all the wine-filled glasses, that is, he could drink at will or he could make suggestions to the Underboss on inviting other players to share the drinks. The Underboss could also make suggestions as to who should be given a drink. The Boss could accept the suggestion or reject it. Sometimes the Boss and Underboss consumed all the drinks. When a player was offered a drink, he could not refuse it.

The real object of the game was to offer no drinks to one participant for the entire evening (going dry), while offering too many drinks to another player until he was drunk. Each evening was fun-filled, watching one frustrated person who had nothing to drink for the entire evening while another player was slurring his words and weaving from side to side by the evening's end.

Virginia Mesolella Graf

∞ **Rest Hour** ∞

I walked past
the 13th Century Romanesque church
along the dusty pebble path
until I reached the heavy
wooden door of the piccolo *museo*.
A workman in overalls
sitting under a tree
smoking a cigarette
waved his hands at me
and shouted, *"Restauro!"*
"Oh, rest hour," I mumbled out loud,
turning around
and heading toward the piazza
a half mile away.
At a caffe' I nursed a bottle
of *acqua frizzante*
wrote postcards
musing on the similarities
of Milan to the South of Italy:
In the South work stopped
in the afternoon for siesta time
while in Milan
Italy's modern commercial hub
work stopped for rest hour.
After letting ninety minutes lapse
I walked back to the *museo*
and again the workman waved me away
saying, "Restauro!"
"Rest hour, my ass!" I snarled
pointing to my watch,
"it's going on two hours!"
Looking puzzled,

the workman signaled for me to wait
then disappeared in the doorway
returning with a calendar.
He flipped through the pages,
"Gennaio, febbraio, marzo,
aprile, maggio, e luglio
– sei mesi,"
he said holding up his fingers,
"Restauro!"
What game is he playing, make a fool out
of the American tourist?
I said to myself.
Let him take rest hours
for six months or six years
for all I care as I
shook my head and left.
Back at my pensione
I was cursing out
the Italian lifestyle
when my English speaking host
explained that *restauro*
meant work restoration.

Gil Fagiani

Across Generations

The Spizzirri Family Odessy: From Italy to America

∞ The Spizzirri Family Odyessy: From Italy To America ∞

To transplant my mother's family, the Spizzirri family, from Marano Marchesato, province of Cosenza, Calabria, to the United States took nearly a century. It involved numerous trips between the small southern Italian village and the New World, made by a score of relatives. It involved civil court proceedings, hearings, and accusations of fraud. It was interrupted by two world wars and a global economic depression. In the end, most of the Spizzirri family made a home for themselves in America. A few returned to Marano Marchesato to start businesses with American-made money. And a few stayed in Italy, never venturing to join their cousins in the New World.

It began with my great-grandfather, Giacomo Spizzirri. Born in Marano Marchesato in 1869, he was a large man, about 5'9" according to his Italian draft registration notice, much taller according to his grandchildren. He had gray, close-set eyes and large, strong hands. The Spizzirris had been shepherds since at least the mid-1700s. And, in post-unification Calabria, their poverty was keenly felt.

Beginning in the 1880s, *Maranesi* villagers, mostly men, had journeyed to America where they hoped to find work quickly and earn sufficient money to return to Italy and provide for their families in relative comfort.

In 1889, Giacomo married Raffaela Sicilia. By early 1891, Raffaela was pregnant with their first child, and Giacomo joined the growing number of *Maranesi* who were heading to America. Like his *paesani* before him, he made his way to Chicago where he found work on the railroad section gangs, laying new rails and repairing existing track. He made two round trips in the 1890's, each time working on railroads between Chicago and the northwestern prairie.

At some point, and for some reason, he decided to obtain United States citizenship. He was granted citizenship in a circuit court in Chicago in October 1894. There may have been some irregularity involved in Giacomo's procurement of U.S. citizenship. In 1894, he surely hadn't lived in the U.S. the requisite five years. In any event, he walked out of the courthouse as a United States citizen, with all the corresponding rights and privileges. By the laws of the day, his entire family, which included two children born in Italy while he was in America, now enjoyed derivative United States citizenship. He returned to Italy in July 1899.

In early 1901, with Raffaela expecting their third child, Giacomo sailed again for Chicago. In May, his son (my grandfather) Mariano was born; like the rest of his family, Mariano acquired derivative United States citizenship. Giacomo returned to Italy in 1905, but made the trip to Chicago again in 1906, this time with his twelve-year-old son Michele, who would work as a water boy next to his father on the railroad section gang. The two stayed in America until 1911. In early 1913, Giacomo returned to Chicago with both his sons, all three traveling as United States citizens. They returned to Italy in 1915, and their sojourns were put on hold due to World War I.

The Spizzirris' resumed their transatlantic travel in the 1920s. Giacomo's sons, like their father, started families in Italy while working in America. Giacomo's last stay in America was from 1922 to 1924, when he returned to Marano Marchesato permanently; however, he was still an American citizen. Giacomo would appear before U.S. consulates in Italy with his naturalization certificate, annotated and stamped, creased, torn, and taped, and carried in his pocket during many round trips between Italy and Chicago, in order to prove that his sons and his daughters - in - law were entitled to derivative American citizenship and, therefore, American passports. In the late 1920s, this aroused the suspicion of consulate officials in Messina, and Giacomo's papers were confiscated. After some court proceedings, in 1929 his citizenship was canceled on the grounds of fraud. Suddenly, and unbeknownst to them, his children were no longer American citizens. Giacomo, living in Italy, was perhaps unaware of the outcome of the legal proceedings taking place against him in America, and did not inform his sons in Chicago.

In the meantime, my grandfather lived and worked in Chicago and Kenosha, Wisconsin, throughout the 1920s and 1930s. As an American citizen, or so he thought, he made a trip back to his family in Italy during that time. In 1939, my grandfather began the paperwork to bring his entire family, consisting of his wife, Giuseppina, and children Bellina, Giacomo, Valentino, and Eva, all American citizens, or so he thought, to America. Immigration officials, upon checking the status of Mariano's derived citizenship, found that Giacomo's citizenship had been revoked and that, therefore, the citizenship of Mariano and his family was in question.

What followed was an onslaught of correspondence between and among the numerous government agencies involved in immigration and citizenship. Government lawyers wrote to government officials who in turn sought clarification amid growing cross-references and file numbers; eventually, the cascade of correspondence trickled down to my grandfather, a poor factory laborer and, he thought, an honest American citizen. Although he had minimal schooling in Italy, my grandfather was by no means an illiterate man. Still, he sought help from the traditional go-betweens who lived in all Italian American communities during this era; eventually he hired an Italian American lawyer. After numerous hearings and voluminous correspondence, he was denied permission to bring his family to America. He was declared to be an illegal alien; never mind that he had traveled between America and Italy three times as an American citizen; never mind that he had voted in every American election. Thus deprived of his former citizenship status, he began application for U.S. citizenship. The wheels of bureaucracy turned slowly, so slowly that weeks turned into years and allies turned into enemies. By the end of 1942, with America at war with Italy, my grandfather, who had lived most of his life as an American citizen and was in fact registered and eligible for the military draft, was arrested on the charge of being in the United States without a proper visa. Fortunately, cooler, more logical heads prevailed, and, in 1944, he was allowed to journey to Windsor, Canada, for one day; he reentered the United States at Detroit, via the Detroit-Canada tunnel, on a pre-approved visa. He then began regular citizenship application proceedings. These proceedings were finally finished, and my grandfather became a full-fledged American citizen in 1949.

But the damage had been done. My grandmother, mother, and uncle, all once legitimate American citizens, weren't able to join my grandfather until 1947, eight years after Mariano's initial request. My other uncle and his family couldn't come to Kenosha until 1950 and 1951. Other descendants of Giacomo journeyed to Chicago and to Canada in the 1950s. And my aunt Bellina finally made the trip to America in 1966, coming with her sons to work in Kenosha with an eye to returning to Italy and living in relative comfort. In the early 1970 s, they did return and,by the early 1990s, they opened a pizzeria, *gelateria*, and bar in Marano Marchesato. Thus, in Italy and America, the family had completed the process begun by my great-grandfather Giacomo Spizzirri in 1891.

Peter L. Belmonte

∞ Cugino Mio: Prince of the City ∞

Valledolmo, Sicily is a town of forty-five hundred people, which lies about thirty miles southeast of Palermo. Set in the mountains, it is the ancestral home of most of the Italian Americans who were born and raised in Fredonia, New York. As a special event for the three dozen Fredonians on our tour of Italy in October of 1997, a chartered bus from Palermo met us in Agrigento and drove us to Valledolmo. It would return us to Palermo by nightfall, when we would rejoin the rest of the tour.

I had no reason to suspect that I had relatives in Valledolmo. My paternal grandfather was born in Carda, Sicily and my maternal grandparents were reared in Valguarnera di Caropepe, Sicily. Still, I was excited about going to Valledolmo, in part because of the contagious enthusiasm of the many Fredonians who did have relatives there.

After a treacherous drive up the mountains through the narrow winding roads, we arrived at our destination. We were met in the town's center by dozens of smiling Valledolmese. As I was leaving the bus, I heard the refrain "Belliotti" (Bell- ee- owe- tee in Italian). I was stunned. Apparently someone had sent a copy of the names of those of us who were arriving. And someone was bellowing my name. Margaret Valone, who was the first off the bus pointed to me. I stepped off the bus gingerly and was confronted by a sharp-featured woman, about age sixty-five. She peered at my name tag and asked, "Bell-ee-owe-tee?" I introduced myself as "Ray Belliotti." She looked quizzically at the "Ray." She seemed to be thinking, "What the blazes is a 'Ray'?" I recovered quickly and said, "Rosario," the name of my paternal grandfather after whom

I was named. In the United States, everyone called him "Ray."

She smiled expansively, nodding in an acceptance I would only understand later in the day. She introduced herself as "Maria Stefania Belliotti." Bingo! It sounded like relative-city to me. The name "Belliotti" is very rare in Italy and the United States.

Suddenly, from out of the shadows, emerged another Belliotti, Rosolino, a tall man, balding, aquiline featured who looked younger than his fifty-five years. He looked more like the Florentine nobleman one sees depicted in Renaissance murals than the Sicilian laborers from whom I had sprung. He extended his hand, smiled warmly but suspiciously, and led me toward Valledolmo's town hall where a major conclave between the Fredonians and their Sicilian relatives was about to begin. After about an hour the local priest ended the program in the town hall with a prayer and a summary of the day's events: a tour of historical sites culminating with a wine tasting, a feast prepared by the locals for the tourists, and a benediction ceremony in one of the city's beautiful churches.

I was preparing to join the crowd, but that was not going to happen. The resolute will of Rosolino Belliotti interceded. He unraveled a long scroll which had Belliotti genealogy dating back two centuries. His message was clear: prior to wasting time on me he had to be assured that I fit into the family tree. I asked Sal Crino, a native Sicilian who had emigrated to the United States in 1958, to be my translator. Then Sal, Rosolino, Maria Stefania, and I went to the town hall, and sat down at a table to figure out from what branch of the Belliotti tree I had sprung. They told me that the Belliottis had originated in Tuscany, arriving in Sicily in the 1700s.

It took about forty-five minutes. Most of the others had already left the town hall. Less determined people would have given up, but Rosolino Belliotti had not achieved what he had —he turned out to be a medical doctor and was one of the wealthiest people in the town — by surrendering in the face of adversity, Mercifully, the Sicilian tradition of naming the first-born after the paternal grandfather is a tremendous aid to aspiring genealogists. Coincidentally, my father, my grandfather, and I are all first sons.

So how were Rosolino, Maria Stefania and I related? My great-grandfather and their great-grandfather were brothers. I believe that makes us fourth cousins (or maybe 3 1/2 cousins). *Cugino! Cugina!* After this discovery, they treated me like a brother or son who had just returned from the war.

Now Rosolino swept into action. Quickly he separated me from the crowd. His message: you are a Belliotti, kid. We don't follow the herd. He stormed into a store, bought me two postcards of Valledolmo, and stuffed them in my pocket. He corralled Sal Crino to act as my interpreter.

We went to the family home, which just happened to be an historical landmark, the oldest, and apparently largest, home in Valledolmo. He introduced me to his wife, an effusive woman who was one of the few heavyset women I saw in Italy. The highlight, however, was a closed off portion of the house formerly occupied by Rosolino and Maria Stefania's father, Francesco. It was more of a palazzo than a home with beautiful murals, mosaics, and priceless antiques. I was shown numerous old family photos. Everything was happening so fast I had a difficult time focusing. But one thing was clear – Rosolino had fancied himself as prince of the city.

It was time to eat, Rosolino declared. I half expected manna to fall from heaven upon the order of the prince of the city. Nothing that dramatic occurred but we entered the restaurant – after all, it would have been too herdlike to meet everyone else to partake of the town's especially

155 / Across Generations

prepared feast. Rosolino and Sal conferred on a menu. And the good times started to roll.

The meal was the saga of an overly assimilated Italian American who has long forgotten the tricks of old world dining, a sly fox named Sal, and generous but demanding hosts – *miei cugini*. We ate for what seemed hours. Later as I waddled out of the restaurant Rosolino again took the lead. We traveled to the house of another sister, Pina, I think. Our relatively short visit included strong, black Sicilian coffee, and another photo session.

Finally, after a ride in Rosolino's car, which was almost too big for the narrow streets, we rejoined the Fredonians at a wine-tasting at the local winery. It felt good to enjoy the group's enthusiasm and good will. But even here, Rosolino was compelled to travel a different path. He asked the owner to show us the fermenting wine. Sal, Rosolino and I climbed a dangerous, spiraling ladder. Reaching the top we were forced to crouch to avoid a low ceiling. In a long vat, the purple juice bubbled with a rhythmic beat. The odor was intoxicating.

Even in church, as the priest gave the concluding benediction and religious gifts were presented to the Fredonians, Rosolino went his own way. Taking me with him, we visited various parts of the old church. In the new church, he pointed out the features of this magnificent edifice. In the sacristy there was a full mural of a Belliotti gracing a wall. This Belliotti ancestor was a priest who allegedly performed several miracles and almost achieved sainthood. A holy Belliotti!

That I had a Belliotti ancestor in heaven who might be able to pull a few strings gave me confidence as I prepared to board the tour bus to Palermo, with my group. Just prior to departing I asked Margaret Valone to tell Rosolino's wife and Maria Stefania that "I came to Valledolmo as a stranger but I leave with you in my heart."

Their hospitality was overwhelming. Margaret broke down and cried. It touched her. I insisted she translate. She pulled herself together and relayed the message. The ladies were also touched and kissed me. I was thrilled to end such a wonderful day on a positive note. But there was still Rosolino to deal with.

Although it was time to leave, he clearly had more on his agenda. I begged him to let me board the bus, which was now idling menacingly. He disappeared, then returned to present me with a gift-wrapped, three bottle, set of Valledolmo wine. Wow! The prince of the city set himself off from the crowd again. I thanked him profusely, clutched my gift tightly and merged into the crowd pushing its way onto the bus. What a day! It felt good to be a Belliotti.

Raymond A. Belliotti

∞ Bella Sicilia ∞

Sicily – Friday, 30 July 1998. The journey from Toronto through Rome to Catania, Sicily, with my son Dominic, seemed to take forever. When we were warmly greeted by my cousins at the airport, my weariness ended – we were with family again. After being processed through customs we loaded into the car that was waiting for us and headed for Brucoli. It is a small town on the Mediterranean where my father-in-law, Dominic Grasso, was born. His brother, Francesco and his family have a small summer home there, near the beach. Most of the first day was spent reacquainting ourselves with cousins, eating and drinking wine, which was continuously offered, while the word spread that my son and I had arrived.

Brucoli remains much as it was hundreds of years

earlier. The major industries are fishing and tourism. The pure, clear water is the number one attraction for swimmers and boaters. The landmark, *Castello di Regina Giovanna* sits at the tip of the peninsula. A queen of Spain constructed this small fortress centuries ago, when Spain had occupied the territory.

During July and August the normal Brucoli population of five hundred grows to more than two thousand, not including the young people who come into the area each evening from various parts of Sicily for the well known night life. The main streets were blocked off to accommodate the people strolling in the warm evening air. I had the sense of acceptance and belonging as we walked along a crowded street to the piazza.

The purpose of our trip to Sicily with my son Dominic was, primarily, to visit my wife's relatives. In addition to her Uncle Francesco Grasso and his wife, we were expecting to visit cousins Sebastiano and Antonina Verderame and their relatives who resided in Caltinessetta. We also planned to be in Montedoro for a week staying with cousins Giuseppe and Pina Saia. My parents were born in Montedoro, and if the opportunity presented itself, I wanted to conduct some basic genealogical research on my family.

Prior to arriving in Montedoro, however, we were treated to a banquet-style reunion with relatives in Brucoli, and again in Caltinessetta. We got off the train in Montedoro the night before the Festa di San Giuseppe was due to begin. At 6 a.m. the next morning the eleven loud cannon bursts reminded us that church services were beginning that would announce the official opening of the Festa. For the week-long event we were treated to a procession honoring the patron saint, a spectacular fireworks display in the piazza, musical bands serenading people during the evening hours, dancing in the streets, and booths of games, food, and desserts.

The conversations that people of Montedoro had with us invariably ended with their either being related on my mother's side (Mantione) or my father's side (Licata) of the family. We enjoyed the many hours of conversation with them. The day after the Festa ended Dominic and I decided to begin our search of family records. We found the assistance provided by Padre Amadeo of La Chiesa Santa Maria del Rosario to be most helpful. From the church's registry he wrote out a copy of my parent's wedding certificate. Here we also were able to validate the ancestry ledger back to my fifth, great grandfather, to the mid 1700s. Much to our surprise, there was a new name not previously known, one that we had not previously encountered. My fifth great grandfather's name was Leonardo Licata Gallina. The surname had apparently been dropped by my third grandfather. So that's how I became a Licata!

We had been visiting with Padre Amadeo for more than two hours. Now it was time for his *pranzo* and his afternoon siesta. We were so excited that we returned later that same afternoon to the church. Thanks to Dominic's genealogy program on his Macintosh laptop computer, we discovered an error on the year of my parents' wedding. The certificate stated that they were married in 1918, but I knew that my oldest sister was born in Montedoro in 1910. The good padre brought my parents back to respectability by finding that they were married in 1908. Whoever had transcribed the record into the registry, which was in Latin, had mistakingly entered the year of the wedding as 1918. We all had a good laugh as the padre cancelled out the old date on the certificate and inserted the correct one.

It is said that many of the farmers who had inhabited Montedoro two to three hundred years ago were born in one of several neighboring towns. We inquired at the oldest church in nearby Serradifalco which is the repository for old records of the region. The ledgers for the years preceding 1750 had been found by its pastor in a damp, unused part of the church. They are in such terrible shape that the ink has faded to near invisibility. The padre plans to resurrect these ledgers into the computer when he is able. We have reason to believe that centuries ago both sides of my family may have resided in another nearby town, Racalmuto. Maybe another trip to Sicily soon?

Don Licata

∞ In Celebration of a Well Lived Life ∞

It is for you Grandma that I write, and your extended family
who did not welcome your departure from this earthly plane
on February 28 in the year of our Lord 1981,
the same month another great lady,
Governor Ella Grasso of Connecticut,
passed away.

You were more a Queen Mother to us;
born out of strife to Luigi and Rosa from Salerno
Angelina Consolmagno,
you were a Survivor
of poverty, the Spanish influenza, rickets as a child,
epilepsy, and several bouts of pneumonia,
to flourish past your birthplace on Mulberry Street, New York City
and become mother to many
at 2056 West Fifth Street, Brooklyn,
where I spent my early childhood years.

Your first husband, Giovanni Falci, died at 25
during the terrible epidemic that took many young lives
and he tried to take you and your infant child along too,
but you said, no, we choose life and called your brothers in
to stop him from turning on the gas light.
You moved on to make pretty hats and accessories to raise
your child,
march with the suffragettes for women's rights
along Fifth Avenue one of your spots on earth,
before you remarried my Grandfather, Rocco,
and raised his three children like they were your own,
orphaned by the same dread disease,
later to have Rosie, my mother,
and the only child born of that union.

I can remember the world passing by your porch windows,
filled with local color, all types of visitors you welcomed in
and entertained
as well as our closely knit tribe:
Uncle Vinney and Aunt Fay, and cousin Rocky, my favorite
guy,
were beside you, above, Uncle Nicky, Aunt Anne, their
children Anthony and
Annie, while up the street lived your Uncle Lew and his
wife Clara.
Rose, Joe, my father, and Aunt Anna were nestled there
with you and Pop
as they referred to Grandpa
in our big duplex, huge as the universe to my childish eyes
not too far from Coney Island,
the seacoast where I frolicked and played
when it was still beautiful.

We will never forget the taste of your savory food.
Only the lucky few knew your homemade raviolis,
marinara sauces or roasted peppers and grispels

the way that I do;
pure and nourishing foods, patiently created for us.
Your grandson Anthony said it best,
"Gram, we're selfish; 88 years were not enough!"
We know you are in a heavenly light,
 but we are still here in our earthly plight
Without your stories, joyous sense of humor,
so full of life, a peace-maker in our time.

Angie, some called you, Angela, Angelina,
"Little Angel," you were our giant, a legendary figure
though you felt so small at only 4' 10" tall.
Grandma, did you really think your work was done
after all the years of tenderly caring for us?
God/dess knows that you deserved the rest,
but oh how we miss your quiet presence.
Angela, my sister, bears your name
and what a name it is: tigress, woman of strength,
teacher of independence, "even from the men."
You set the standard with your step
as we witnessed your courage and contentment
even during the worst of times, you smiled and toasted life
with your favorite red wine, dancing all the while,
right until the end
when you called us one by one
to say good-bye,
finally telling Rosie,
"I'm tired of washing, mending the socks
and I don't feel for shelling the peanuts."

Quietly you left that day
when the flowers bloomed in February
and the bees buzzed for a short while.
Uncanny many people said, a false spring,
we were not surprised.
I, myself, saw the fairies dancing

at your graveside, dear Grandma.
As you lived, so you reside
in peace, in love and eternal light.

Louisa Calio

∞ Three Generations ∞

After graduating from College in 1970, I was conscripted into military service during the Vietnamese War. I was ideologically opposed to that war for all the usual reasons offered at the time. So what was I to do? Refuse to take the dramatic step forward that signaled acquiescence to military service and subject myself to criminal prosecution? Disavow military service, leave the country, and adopt a persona of a lightweight fugitive? Remain in the country but go underground to escape prosecution? Or bite the bullet, accept induction, and cope with intense internal conflict between deeply held ideology and practical behavior?

In pondering these questions, I was not the least concerned about the prospects of killing or being killed. I knew that if I entered the armed forces that I would enlist, and given my education and academic skills, would probably be assigned a non-infantry role. After much pondering, I decided that I would disavow military service, enter a graduate program in Canada, and apply for landed immigrant status there.

My father howled. We had the worst arguments of our lives. My father's opposition to my decision stemmed not from ideology or morality – he thought the war rather stupid and pointless – but on strict prudence: if I left the country I could never return without being subject to capture and criminal prosecution. Weaned on too many episodes of *The Fugitive*, I was convinced that I could easily outwit the authorities and be able to come and go as I pleased, whereas my father was equally convinced that someone in our small town would enthusiastically give me up. The problem was compounded by the failing health of my mother that would seemingly impair her or my father's ability to visit me in Canada.

Just prior to my departure, however, my father came into my bedroom, tossed a set of keys on the bed, and growled,

"You'll need these for your trip." That is all he said.

The keys belonged to an automobile, a Cutlass; he had purchased it for me. This gesture was typical of my father's instinctive generosity in the face of a situation that could not be resolved without conflict. I cried that day. I think he may have, too.

I went to Canada and applied for landed immigrant status. I enrolled in a graduate program in philosophy to which I had been accepted and began the unsettling process of learning a new, but not a radically different culture. Events were soon to conspire against me. My mother's health degenerated and it became clear that any appreciable separation from her was out of the question.

After only a few weeks in Canada, I returned to the United States. I enlisted in the army and was deemed qualified for military intelligence. I served almost three years, most of which was in Washington, DC and Korea. I have never regretted my original decision to go to Canada, or my decision to return and serve in the military.

Almost twenty years later, on October 15, 1992, I presented "Columbus and the Italian Americans" at a *Conversations Across the Faculty Forum* held at the State University of New York at Fredonia to mark the five-hundredth anniversary of Columbus' landing in the Americas. At the end of my presentation, after the obligatory polite applause, the squeals of a thin, high-pitched voice resounded in the four hundred-seat theater. My son, Angelo, who was then four years old, had jumped out of his seat and yelled, "That's my daddy!" It was the proudest and most gratifying moment of my life.

Raymond A. Belliotti

Food and Drink

Mama the Gourmet Cook

∞ Mamma the Gourmet Cook ∞

Our parents were Italian immigrants. They had five children, four boys and a girl. Our mother, Rose, was born in 1903 in Peschici, Italy, a small mountain village overlooking the Adriatic Sea. Mamma immigrated to the U. S. at the age of sixteen to work as a domestic in the household of her uncle Luigi and his wife. She was sent to this country against her will because there wasn't enough money to sustain her family. She was expected to send money back home, which she dutifully did for many years thereafter. She never had the desire to return to Italy because she did not want to be reminded of the poverty that existed when she lived there. It evoked too many painful memories. Papa was born in 1896 in Valledolmo, Sicily. He was a young boy when his father died. He came to this country in 1914 along with his mother and two older sisters.

Among our favorite memories of growing up in Rochester, New York in the 50's are Sunday mornings. We came home after church to the wonderful smell of tomato sauce simmering on the stove, the radio tuned to WSAY, Atillio Iacelli's longest running radio program – "Italian Musicale," and my mother making *pasta di casa* on the kitchen table. She'd be frying meatballs, sausage, pork, bracciola, and veal for the sauce, which made the combined aromas intoxicating. We invariably sampled the sauce by dunking pieces of fresh bread from the Rochester Bakery on Goodman Street. We would also snatch one or two meatballs from the sauce pan to tide us over until the sumptuous feast that would be served precisely at noon.

No meal would be complete at our house on Rustic Street off Clifford Avenue (on Rochester's East Side), without our father's homemade wine. Every two years our house would smell of fermenting Muscato grapes as Papa made a dry white wine that was his pride and joy. During the wine making ritual in our basement, each of the boys was asked to stick their head into the barrel to take in the wonderful odor of fermenting grapes and juice, whereby we immediately became intoxicated by the fumes. Papa would provide a hearty laugh at this event.

We were introduced to wine at an early age. At dinner time, it was the duty of the youngest in the family to go down to the wine cellar to fill a Log Cabin maple syrup bottle with wine for that meal's consumption. Anyone who came to visit our home was treated to a glass of homemade wine, and our father would feign being offended if his offer of a glass of wine was refused. Papa didn't know about enabling alcoholics.

Nobody left mamma's table hungry. There was always enough food to feed six more people. Dropping in uninvited at mealtime was no problem and, indeed, was expected. Meals were times of celebration and camaraderie. All were expected to engage in animated conversation. Being on a weight loss diet was considered sacrilegious. Mamma was a consummate cook who delighted in preparing course after course of the finest food. We were poor but Mamma never scrimped on food. Fresh seasonal fruits included pomegranates, prickly pears, dates and figs. Her favorite expression was, *"Mangia miei figli, mangia!!"* – Eat my children, eat! Fast foods and frozen meats were out of the question. Papa refused to eat meat that had been frozen. Mealtimes lasted approximately four hours. Our father also had a favorite expression at dinner time, *"Non si invecchia, quando mangia"* – one doesn't age while eating a meal.

Every Saturday morning, except in winter, Mamma and Papa went to the public market on Union Street, usually with one of us in tow. They purchased live chickens, fruits, pork butts for making Italian sausage, vegetables, a whole salami, capicolla, Romano and Pecorino cheese, and baby lambs at Easter time. On the way home, stopping at Lanovara's bakery was necessary to purchase a few loaves of Italian bread, cookies, or pastries. In summer we would be treated to a heaping cone of Italian ice which cost a dime. After arriving home Mamma would proceed to kill and clean the chickens while papa made the sausage. If we purchased a baby lamb, we had a pet for the next several days, until shortly before Easter dinner, when our wooly friend mysteriously disappeared! Holiday meals were very special. They consisted of antipasto, soup, ravioli, or some other kind of homemade pasta, a leg of lamb, chicken, or pork, potatoes, vegetables like stuffed artichokes, cardunes, fennel, salad, nuts, chestnuts, fruits and all kinds of homemade and purchased pastries. Calories and cholesterol be damned! And, homemade wine. Grown-ups ate in the dining room, and because of space limitations, kids in the kitchen. How proud the oldest grandchild was when it was his or her turn to graduate to the dining room.

No one could make homemade pasta like my mother She was happiest when preparing food. Her Christmas delicacies of crespelle, pignolata, woochidati, and guandi, were scrumptious. We can still taste them fifty years later. No recipe was ever used. It was a pinch of this and a handful of that – and yet everything turned out delicious. Trying to cook like my mother was impossible, as her daughters-in-law discovered, because of her inexact methods of measuring.

My mother died in 1979 but she lives on in our memory. She was the quintessential Italian Mamma who epitomized unconditional love. A photo of her with a big smile on her face dropping ravioli into a pot of boiling water is permanently affixed to our refrigerator door. The same photo is displayed in the kitchens of the homes of all of her other children.

Anthony Sciolino and Marian Pellegrino

∞ The House of Spirits ∞

In addition to making wine, during prohibition, Papa also made his own alcohol. Once a year he set up a miniature still over the bathtub – the only available space in our fourth-floor walk up in East Harlem in New York City. Since the alcohol making process usually lasted several days, taking a bath was impossible during this period. So we washed as best we could in the kitchen sink. A small price to pay to watch fermented sugar and raisins in the huge copper kettle being heated over a low flame until steam escaped from the spout of the kettle and passed through narrow copper tubing on its way to the cooler. Then the greatest fascination — the slow but steady drip of the distilled liquid as it transformed into pure alcohol. Miniature bottles containing essences – concentrated flavors of various liqueurs – were purchased and mixed with the alcohol to produce Crème de Menthe, Anisette, Crème de Cacao, Grenadine, Strega, and other popular liqueurs. Any leftover alcohol was put aside to preserve Bing cherries when they became available. Though we may have been lacking in money and the simple comforts of life, we were never lacking in "spirits." These concoctions were made solely for our family's use, no bottle ever left our apartment.

Our immigrant parents taught us to hold our American teachers in the highest regard; respect bordered on reverence. This notion of unconditional obedience nearly wreaked havoc on our simple home when I was a first grader and feeling quite important after having graduated from kindergarten. The incident was the result of a hygiene lesson during which we were instructed on the importance of a weekly tub bath.

"But I can't take a bath this week." I told the teacher

after having flagged down her attention with a high waving hand.

"And why not?" she asked.

"Because my father is using the bathtub to make alcohol."

The stunned look on my teacher's face assured me of having well presented a plausible excuse for not bathing. Pleased with myself, I took my seat.

Several days later the still was dismantled, the making of alcohol completed. Our family sat around the kitchen table having dinner when heavy footsteps up the long flight of stairs were followed by loud pounding on our apartment door.

"Who is it?" Papa asked.

"Open up. It's the police," came the gruff reply.

Upon witnessing the domestic scene of three children huddled around parents, each of whom cradled an infant, the plain clothes men relaxed their tone.

"We heard about a disturbance in an apartment across the alley whose rear window faces yours and we're checking it out."

Papa led them the few steps into the bedroom and opened the window. They barely glanced out. Returning to the kitchen, they humbly apologized for disturbing our dinner and left us shaking like a leaf.

Now my parents were not so naïve as to believe the detectives' story. Later that night as I lay in bed hugging my favorite doll, I overheard my parents, in the kitchen, talking to each other in Italian.

"But who could have told them about making alcohol?" Mamma asked.

Like the wedding guest in the *Rime of the Ancient Mariner,* I arose the next day "a sadder and wiser" girl.

Viola Medori Labozzetta

∞ Pasta e Piselli: Lunchtime Memories ∞

Pasta e piselli   piselli e pasta
a simple lunch   poor people's feast

during the second world war
your Aunt Domenica and I were alone

  in Sicily

  the Germans in town
  the Americans advancing

your grandfather in New Jersey
an enemy land   no letters allowed
he'd sent for his sons just before the war
I knew my sons were fighting for the Americans

your aunt and I were alone
      and often hungry

Put the garlic and olive oil and some onion in the pan
    when they're golden throw in the peas
    fresh or frozen whatever you have
    add some water let them cook
    throw in the basil, salt, pepper if you like
    a little parsley

the miseria got so bad
winters were the worst
all we had to eat were onions, olives

some dried fruit, a little wine
   forget about the pasta
   hard then to even make bread
the grain was on the trains heading for Germany

I had no brothers, no sisters
   my parents were dead
all alone your aunt and I

once I heard there was contraband meat
I walked seven chilometers
to get a piece as big as a baby's fist
   for your aunt
she was thirteen, had to grow, had to develop

I roasted that tough little piece for her
   watched her eat
I ate a few olives, drank some wine
she wanted to give me some
No I said you're growing
   you need it
   I'm already grown
I never had much taste for meat
I never eat it now

So, now we put water on to boil
   for the pasta
check the peas, let them simmer
they smell good, no?
   poor people's feast
   pasta e piselli
   piselli e pasta

Those days during the war

the cat was eating soap
she was so hungary
not even enough birds or mice to eat
such miseria

I had a little money put aside
but I couldn't buy a thing
I went to buy grain once
the man said there was none
I noticed one speck of golden wheat
    on the floor
I covered it with my foot stood there
    as people came in
    went away with hungry hearts
when no one else was there
    I said Signore, you have grain
    I have a piece under my foot
He begged me not to report him to the fascists
    he gave me a small bag
    I never told
we had a little bread for a while
I burned rags when I baked it so nobody knew

You can cut us some bread
    from this nice loaf
    the water is boiling
    I put in the pasta
I like little shells, penne, fusilli
    but any pasta is good

When I came here to my husband's house
    in 1946
here was this stove
no more walking for wood
no more kindling a flame

just turn a knob, blue flame, a miracle

The Germans were finally chased out
one day we saw American soldiers
    riding into town
 I cried to see that flag
 carried by those rowdy young men
    that all the young women
    were kissing and cheering
I kept my daughter close
hid her as I did from the Germans
    but those boys could've been my sons
    riding in a jeep
    somewhere in the world

Let's take the pasta down
    we drain it
put the peas in with the pasta
mix it up good, put it in the dishes
grate the cheese over the pasta
    piselli e pasta
pasta e piselli

Wash the cherries
we'll have fruit afterwards

we had our own cherry trees in Sicily
when we ate cherries in the summertime
    we got healthy

one day your aunt and I
went to pick our cherries
American soldiers sat in our trees
    eating cherries

your aunt was angry
    chase them away, Mamma
I told her
    let them eat   let them enjoy
    maybe somewhere my sons are hungry
    and there are cherry trees for them

The Madonna saved us all
    from the war

we have had our feast
pasta e piselli,   piselli e pasta
    fruit, too

a simple lunch
poor people's feast.

Maria Fama

∞ L'Americana ∞

    I gotta nicey restipe data my sista Maria she giva to me. The Americani dey maka soma good food, and my sista she gotta restipe from her fren. She maka pond cake. Oh, my kids dey love dissa pond cake. I likey, too. It'sa pond cake and somma whoop cream. But, I maka lika we maka cake inna Sant' Ambrigio. You gotta putta justa leetle bitta liqwore inna, to maka taste betta. My husband he likey da anisetta, so I usa anisetta. Then you gotta putta da ryeberries – fresh, anna sweet. Oh, it'sa good. My kids dey wanna I makey. I tella my leetle girl, "You come by me. We taka da bus and we go to a marketa and we buy somma ryeberries."
    And we shoppa. I taka da banani becos we eata lotsa

dem. I taka carciofi – becos dey looka good. I taka spinaci, broccoli, e zucchini. I gonna maka nicey Parmigiana witta zucchini, maybe. Ma den I look, I look, ma I canno see da ryeberries. Ma, no! Canno be. I see inna newpape, I gotta coopon. I say to my leetle girl, "You go anna aska da guy. You say, 'Did you gimme please where I canna find da ryeberries?'" She'sa too shy, dissa one. She no wanna go. I don know why my kids dey too shy. I say, "No be too shy! Dissa you country. It'sa no my country. You speak Inglese, so you gotta talk. You no be shy. No try to be ignorante."

Ma all the time she get mad. Den she cry. Justa one look inna face anna she cry. She's too sensitive. Ma you aska nicey an she gonna do. So, I say, "Gioia, please go anna aska da guy," anna she say, "Okay."

So she go anna I wait. She come back anna she'sa crying. I askey, "Why you cry?" She no wanna tell. I getta scare. I tell, "You say to me why! Dis guy he tell you somma ting?" I gotta five girls, anna all da time I worry. You gotta worry becos men canna be *figli di putani* witta leetle girls. Ma she still no wanna say. I shut my mouth. She find da ryeberries. I paya too much anna we go.

We stand by da bus stoppa and she no talk. I come down by her, look inna face and I say, "You gonna say please to me why you cry?" Dissa time she say to me, and den I cry too. She say to me, "Mamma, why you say me askey for ryeberries? You da mamma, but you don know. You suppose teachy me, me no teachy you. You gotta say 'raspberries,' no 'ryeberries.'"

She feela stoopid. She think I stoopid, I know. She cry - I cry. Ma dis no my contry. I no canno teachy Inglese to my kids. I canna teachy cooka da food, anna to be good girl, ma even inna my contry I no go by school. How I gonna teachy Inglese? Ma, I no wanna no more she cry so I say, "One day." I tell, "You gonna go by school and you gonna teachy you mamma good Inglese" – becos she'sa smart dissa leetle one. "See, you teachy da raspberries to me!" I say. Anna I give a kiss.

My kids, dey too sensitiva.

Rose Spinelli

∞ Eating in Old Italy . . . and the Evolution of Food Recipes in America ∞

Not very long ago, in old Italy when life went on at a much slower pace, meals represented an important family event. Traditional customs were respected. At dinner time everybody had to be accounted for; no coming or going from the table was tolerated.

Father sat at the head of the table, a place he never yielded because it was the seat of his authority. Nobody started eating before he did; the signal to eat was when he raised his fork and said *buon appetito!* A loaf of bread had to be on the table because without it the angel of the table would not come.

Mother shuttled between the table and the stove assisted by the eldest daughter or daughters, depending on the size of the family. Boys were not required to help. Unless mother spoiled them, children ate everything that was placed before them. Food was not wasted. Leftovers became part of the next meal because food was both scarce and expensive. Waste was an extravagance and an insult to those who had little or nothing. Dinner was a time for family discussions, or for listening to father's advice or reprimand.

Unless a family was well to do, the everyday meals were simple: bread, pasta, rice, cereals, vegetables and fish were usually consumed. Meat was expensive, generally reserved for Sundays, holidays, or for special occasions.

Bread was baked once a week in the evening, after supper. Mother or the children sifted the flour in a wooden trough. Water, yeast, and salt, never additives or preservatives, were added to the flour and when thoroughly mixed and kneaded, the dough would be cut and formed into loaves, laid on a bed and covered with a woolen blanket for it to leaven. Before dawn the oven would be fired with fagots (small tied bundles of twigs and kindling), and when the loaves were judged to be perfectly leavened they were laid in the oven with a flat wooden paddle. Bread baking did not seem to be a labor, but a feast: an aura of joy and aroma pervaded the home. Small rolls were baked for children, individually marked and considered a treat.

Hot bread invited a snack. Olive oil and oregano poured and spread on chunks of freshly baked bread was simply delicious for breakfast. Bread dough could be spread flat, dimples made by poking a finger into it, and when baked, olive oil would be spread in the dimples. It was called *focaccia* and was brought to America by the Genovese and other Northern Italians. If, before baking it was covered with anchovies, or cheese and tomato bits and oregano, with olive oil poured over it when it came out of the oven, it was *pizza!*

Focaccia or pizza and its ingredients were mother's fantasy. It was essentially, *pane e companatico,* something to go with bread. Italians loved and still love bread well baked, crusty and crunchy. They ate lots of it with *companatico,* such as olives, cheese, salami, mortadella, prosciutto, anchovies and onions. *Pane e formaggio, pan e cipolla,* were expressions denoting scarcity, and poverty. Today these *companatici* are expensive items or gourmet delights.

The G Is returning from Italy brought pizza to America. It soon became popular since it was not only tasty, but also quick to prepare. The Italian pizza went through a process of Americanization. Having cut and spread the dough (enriched with vitamins) to the desired size, a dexterous operator heaves it into the air giving it a spin so that it will gyrate and glide down like a leaf; caught, it is sent again and again into a spin depending upon the number of spectator-customers. The flattened, spun dough is then loaded with salami, ground meat, mushrooms, bacon bits, garlic, onions, drowned in oil and tomato sauce, and sent to the oven. Cooked, it is placed before the customer to be eaten with a fork since it is too soggy to hold. That's *pizza alla' americana!* And that's what a tourist will get in Italy if he doesn't insist, with a truculent face, on the simple pizza that Italians of old used to eat.

So as not to render a meal monotonous, variations were necessary even though the ingredients were still the same. Pasta in all forms prepared in all manners, was the main staple since it was the most nourishing. It was said that pasta filled the void in the stomach. Now experts claim that pasta, because of its slow releasing energy is recommended to athletes, especially joggers.

Rice in Southern Italy was considered a non-nourishing food without sufficient staying power. The reason why Northern Italians ate more rice was because of its availability. Rice grows in abundance in the Po valley, in Piemonte, Lombardia, and the Veneto regions.

There are other variations. Corn mash, *polenta* was largely consumed in the north east section of Italy for the same reason. It often replaced bread. *Pasta e fagioli,* a thick soup of beans and pasta seasoned with olive oil or pork lard was also considered a staple food, rich in proteins. Cereals, such as lentils and chickpeas, were also used in the same fashion. Cooked or raw vegetables were popular, as well.

All these culinary preparations are still popular with families of Italian descent and widely known among non-

Italians. They have undergone variations, motivated mainly by the necessity of time. Many old Italian recipes required time. Spaghetti and meatballs is the outcome of the Italian ragu, a meat sauce that required hours of slow simmering. An American variation is the loading of garlic, spices, and butter, thus rendering food excessively rich.

There is a Sicilian barbecue sauce called *ammogghiu* that means "wrap-up." In Italy it is made by mixing bits of tomatoes, olive oil, garlic, all gently tamped in a marble or wooden pestle so as not to do it violence: salt, pepper and oregano are then added in small quantities. While the meat is on the grill, the sauce is spread on it with a bunch of tied basil stalks. The Italo-American does basically the same thing, but in a fast and modern manner. In a high-speed blender that whirls sharp blades, she places whole tomatoes, double doses of garlic cloves, unsaturated oil, salt, pepper, oregano, and basil. A touch of a button, a swirl, and there you have a homogenized sauce, still called *ammogghiu*.

Such is the evolution of Italian food recipes in America.

Vittorio Re

∞ Three Kitchens? You Must be Kidding! ∞

I was in the produce section of one of those gourmet grocery stores looking for a choice bunch of rabe when I noticed that a tall, golden-haired woman with a fur hat and coat, and very thin red lips was sort of stalking me. She and a shorter man with a ridge of graying hair, in a full-length leather coat, seemed to be monitoring my actions and then huddling to whisper. I didn't feel threatened; I was in a public place, in clear view under the fluorescent lights. But I felt a little like a deer caught in the headlights. After one final deliberation the woman walked resolutely toward me. The man followed.

"What is that?" she asked.

"Rabe," I said.

"Say it again." She turned an ear my way and squinted in concentration.

"Rabe, as in .... Robbie Kennedy." They stared humorlessly.

"It's an Italian vegetable in the broccoli family."

"Oh?" Her eyes did a little dance from my head to my toes and back again. "What does it taste like?"

"Well, it's a little bitter, I guess, but it's really good, especially with lemon and garlic."

Her nose crinkled at the word "bitter." The man must have been her husband because he did it too, at the same time. Then they turned to each other in a moment of shared psychology.

"In what?" she prodded.

"In what?"

"What do you serve it with?" The man came gallantly to her rescue.

"Oh. Well, you can have it with pasta, that's always good. Or you can have it as a side dish. That's what we always did for Christmas."

"What else did you have for Christmas?" they asked simultaneously after doing that thing again. And then I swear they moved toward me as if I had something they wanted.

I stepped back. "Oh, let's see." I counted on my fingers. "Tortellini in brodo, pasta al forno, stuffed artichokes, veal Milanese, saltimbocca. And octopus." I said. "We had octopus as an appetizer." As I was switching hands for extra fingers, I saw they were in a kind of swoon. They thanked me, and placed a couple of bunches of rabe in their cart and pushed it away.

They left before I had a chance to tell them about the desserts and about my family's other culinary pursuits. If they'd asked about the octopus I would have explained how it is a holiday specialty and how it's cooked in the garage to spare the house its pungent aroma. We dunk it three times in a pot of boiling water for optimum tenderness and then cook it for about an hour. I'm not sure why three times; this has always been the proscribed way, and we just wouldn't want to stray from tradition.

Next we cut it into small pieces and dunk it again in olive oil, lemon, and oregano with a dash of salt and pepper. We eat it out of a communal platter, while standing. Some of us have favorite parts of the octopus. Because he is the dad and the prime dunker, my father had dibs on the head.

Of all my parents rituals, garage cooking is probably the most difficult to explain. Though it is one of the many time-honored conservation practices, it's not that my family is poor or that the garage is the only room with an electrical outlet. In fact, it's only been within the last couple of decades that they branched out to the garage. Then they went about and equipped it with a stove, refrigerator, freezer, and shelving for pots and spices. It is an attached garage so that the relay of food is easy. They like cooking in the garage, feeling as though they are saving wear and tear on the house. Garage cooking preserves the sanctity of the real kitchen. In fact, my parents have three kitchens: the basement one for everyday use; the regular kitchen, which is pristine but has all the working parts, just like a store display; and the garage, for really big jobs.

The house — and especially the garage — is my family's laboratory, where they nurture their culinary passions. Come to my parent's house anytime, and you'll likely find salamis dangling by their strings from the clothesline, deep in the throes of the aging process, and big cylindrical bricks of homemade ricotta cheese lined up on the laundry room floor. Red peppers and wilting stalks of herbs are hung everywhere. As a child, I was disturbed by these eccentricities. Like any kid my age, all I wanted was peanut butter on white bread with the tiniest suggestion of jelly. Instead, I got homemade bread looking a lot like a football cut on the bias with a zucchini blossom and garlic frittata. I was all too aware that these items did not go unnoticed by the jury of my peers. Every day at lunchtime I suffered through yet another food indignity, pulling out a meatball sandwich bigger than my head, tomato sauce dripping out the sides. There was no way to eat this inconspicuously, so I began stuffing my lunches in places where their aromas began to haunt by midday, perhaps behind the classroom radiator or jammed behind library books at the back of the room. Oh, for a bologna on Wonder Bread!

Things are different now. Kids in restaurants order goat cheese crostini and figs wrapped in prosciutto while their parents look on proudly. But I remember feeling uncomfortably wedged between two worlds. At a sleepover once, a friend's mother made lasagna in honor of the "Italian girl," but she made it with cottage cheese! I quietly phoned home to report the travesty to my mother. Still, whenever I tried to commingle these two worlds I was doomed to crash and burn.

It was my tenth birthday in the fall – tomato canning and wine making season. Up until the day of my party I'm convinced that I will be able to hide the big wine press with its wooden shaft and metal crank and oak casks, from prying eyes of my American friends. It sits near the door where my guests will be arriving. The press looks larger and larger and as I blow up balloons, the smell of fermenting grapes grips my nostrils. I grab a gingham tablecloth and throw it over the behemoth as it sighs and snorts and swells like the machinery behind the Wizard of Oz's billowing curtain. I am a ten-year-old wreck, trying hard to deflect attention from the expanding monstrosity, and keep my guests from entering the other room where there is a carpet of tomatoes being made ready for the cannery. During this time I am asked questions like, "Why do your parents talk so funny?" "Ecoow, what's that?" "What happened to your house?" Looking back, I see clearly that diversity was not practiced then.

It isn't that I resent that things are different today so much as that I haven't fully adapted to the shift. Today my parents could carry on a conversation with Martha Stewart about the subtle differences in taste between the fat-leafed arugula versus the skinny kind. Over the years my taste buds have blossomed. I no longer prefer peanut butter to my parent's gastronomy. And today my sisters and I affectionately refer to one room in my parent's house as "the store." Here one will find bottles of vegetable caponatas, marinated artichoke hearts, black olives in oil, sun-dried tomatoes, and pestos, lots and lots of pestos – all for the taking. Could be worse, I could be buying retail.

But I still carry a free-floating shame about my family being different. Last summer strangers began showing up at my parent's house to look at their garden, which contains vegetables most of us have never heard of. The garden is rather large by neighborhood standards, but to my parents there is never enough space. And so they plant lettuce between the marigolds, tomato plants next to the dahlias. And at the crown of their lawn sits a zucchini plant where most people would plant a rosebush. I was there recently, under the grape arbor sipping espresso, when some strangers came asking questions. I was instantly ten again and an impulse to duck into the house came over me, and yes, I triumphed.

On the other hand, there's the enlightened couple at the gourmet grocery. I spied them at the checkout counter later, where they were discussing with some other shoppers the fancy foods they had in their carts.

"Have you ever eaten rabe?" she asked the strangers.

"It's good with lemon and garlic." He offered.

Rose Spinelli

∞ Fennel ∞
(prose poem)

Too exotic for the Oklahoma of the sixties, "What's this?" the woman at the cash register would ask raising the hairy stalk, her expression half fascination and half disgust, not the way I hoped I would ask what is "collop" or what are collard greens. "What's this?" Oh, I would praise the white flesh, the beautiful hair, the sweet perfume under the shell. I would offer information, plead for the fennell, for its seed: fennel seed tastes good on bread and rolls, cookies, fish, shellfish, I would say; or, try fennel seeds on apples baked with sugar, on top of apple pies, fennel seed with beef, lamb, pork, chicken, and duck, whether stewed or braised, in pilaf and salads and sauerkraut and cheese. I would also plead for fennel shoots: they flavor sauces, soups, chowders, candy, they flavor liqueur, perfume oils, soaps, medications. And blanched, I would add as an afterthought, back home where I come from, everyone knows they can be used in place of celery.

Perennial, relative of carrot and anise, Mediterranean vessel more sealed than an onion, more sealed than a woman's body, grooved, tough outer layer, the hard knot a toothless woman fears under her gums. It's the Florence fennel, finocchio, that seizes my fancy. Finocchio wants to be eaten *al dente*; or if cooked, it's better baked like in

Fennel Parmesan; or, neither raw nor baked, it can be immersed in olive oil with garlic and salt, the dish Florentines call fennel in pinzimonio, sharp-tongued Florentines – always ready to seize the bizarre, always ready to let vulgar usage deform in order to describe - as when they say, "That man is a finocchio," and then they are unkind twice.

"Fennel!" exclaims Natasha, the connoisseur, intent on the pleasure of each ingredient, not unlike listening to a second violin, or suddenly it's the viola shouting at the listener who watches the finger press down the F-string, hears a tremolo, feels the vibration shoot up her arm, head, body, hair.

From Fenelon to Faneuil Hall, the long drawn 'f' feels soothing, a felt tipped pen on paper or a slow-circling falcon on a lazy afternoon, 'f' soft like flannel or like alfalfa tufts a horse lifts from a Vermont field. Fennel. I taste the sound. I hold it like a sigh between my lip and teeth, the sound I release softer than 'shhh'-someone sleeps, precurser of 'n' when I bounce my tongue, hold the tip against the ridge, and wait for the liquid 'l' to fill my mouth.

Sometimes my tongue trips on a vowel. From fennel to funnel, a slight breach or a sudden fracture through which I fall like water down a canyon. I fear the gorge will crush me, food forced down the throat to fatten the Christmas goose, but I save myself as we all do if we open our eyes, foie gras melts in my mouth, an open flue through which smoke curlicues rise, I am an Apache, I read signs, I sniff fumes from a cooking pit, stagger into a new language. Fennel.

Finocchio. There returns the memory of something good, something happy, clean. Another point of view. My first English teacher spoke clear words, simple words as one employs with a child when one wants to be understood. "The body of a women is open," she would say. "Women should not wear skirts. Any thing could enter." Suddenly I am by the Blasha Glass Flowers at Harvard's Botanical Museum. A bumble-bee, a huge bumble-bee – ten, twenty, fifty times its size – hairy legs on a huge fennel flower. Here it is: the mystery of pollination made clear, simple: fruit gestates and is born after the latent labor. And so, new life. And as for fennel, in the Oklahoma of the 1990s, everyone loves fennel like a long lost, newly found language.

Renata Treitel

∞ Sundays Were Special ∞

When I was a young girl my father would walk my brothers and me to our grandparent's house after the nine o'clock Sunday Mass. They were my mother's parents, Saveria Paonessa Mariano and her husband Salvatore Agostino. They lived on the third floor of an apartment house down the street from Saint Joseph's Catholic Church in Niagara Falls, New York. It is the church where my parents Catherine and Rocco Migliazzo were married.

Although many years have passed, I recall, vividly, climbing the stairs to that apartment after church. At the first stair I always took in the aroma of freshly made pasta sauce mingled with the odor of a stogie cigar, most likely a DiNobile, filtering down the long stairway of their apartment. Upon reaching the top step, both grandparents would smother us with the grandest hugs and kisses ever. Taking our faces in their hands, their kisses were so hard I thought I wouldn't have a face left when they were through.

Grandma looked so beautiful in her 4'-11" frame, always attired in a pretty apron over her dress, with a sweet smile on her face and her long white hair pulled back into a bun behind her neck.

Of course the big meal on Sunday was at noon and it was grandma's responsibility to prepare that meal. The meal was always the same, one of which we would never tire because it was so traditional and so delicious. It included homemade sauce, meatballs, home made crunchy bread, wine, and insalata with olive oil and vinegar, served at the end of the meal so as not to interfere with the wine taste. We could also be certain that coffee and espresso along with a baked good from Grandma's oven would be served.

Her specialty, however, was making *polpettine*, literally little meat balls (*polpette*). They were made from a leftover meatball mix. They would be formed into small, flat ovals and browned in olive oil 'til crispy. She usually served them as an appetizer or as a snack. While my father and grandfather drank anisette with coffee, the rest of us ate *polpettine*. How sad that many of these old wonderful traditions have since passed.

Eleanor Migliazzo Novara

∞ Making Cordials ∞

Have you ever tasted a sweet, homemade, alcoholic drink called a "cordial" at an Italian wedding? This drink was served for many years at this celebration but, for the most part, ended in the middle to late fifties. Usually the bride's and groom's father made this delicious, somewhat strong drink, to serve at the newlywed's reception table. I don't know the origin of the word "cordial" but to me it means being friendly, a willingness to please, in a social sense.

My grandfather produced this drink before he passed on in 1952. My father still makes it today. The various flavors he produces include annisette, creme de menthe (green and white), strega, and rosolio. Whenever friends would visit grandpa's house they could depend on being served a tray of grandma's homemade cookies along with a couple of glasses of grandpa's cordials. Making cordials today is a legal practice, but when grandpa made it with bootleg alcohol, I doubt that it was.

In the 1930's, bootleg alcohol was produced in grandpa's neighborhood. When he was in need of a gallon of "hooch," he would place a empty gallon jug and a tablespoon in a paper bag and head for the "distillery" which was located a few short blocks from where he resided. When he arrived, and while in the prescence of the bootlegger, he sampled the alcohol with the spoon, then took a second dip with the spoon, and struck a match to the alcohol in the spoon. If the ignited alcohol produced a light blue glow, grandpa would close the deal and place the full gallon of alcohol in the paper bag. He used this sampling method to verify that the alcohol was of the highest quality.

Instead of using alcohol as the main ingredient to make a cordial, my father uses vodka. His recipe is as follows:

1 - empty, clean, clear, quart-size bottle
20 oz - 80 proof vodka
10 oz. - clear *Karo Syrup*
2 oz. - bottle of your favorite cordial extract (strega, annisette, creme de menthe, etc.).

Extracts may be purchased at a winemaker's supply shop or at an Italian delicatessen/food market.

Mix the vodka, *Karo Syrup*, and the bottle of cordial extract in the quart bottle. Cap the bottle. Shake vigorously for a couple of minutes until the all the ingredients are blended well. Remove the bottle cap and in a small glass, pour yourself your first taste. Enjoy!

Susan Maruggi Stokes

Superstitions, Rituals, and Remedies

Grandma's Ritual

∞ Overlooking ∞

My mother, a second generation Italian American of Neapolitan origin, was a very superstitious woman. She was thoroughly convinced that people could put curses on one another. She called it "overlooking," and that just about everything in life was a matter of good luck or bad luck.

For example, if someone visited our home, one of our family members may have been "overlooked," or cursed during the visit by our guest. After the visitor left, we had to sprinkle salt in the corners of the room and sweep it out the door, taking any curses with it. It was a good thing that we were poor and didn't have carpeting because I don't know if it was allowable to replace a broom with a vacuum cleaner. The curse would probably have remained inside the vacuum cleaner.

One of my favorites was a seasonal ritual. Because March was thought to be a very dangerous month for getting sick, each year on March 1st my mother made my sisters and me take a large sheet of paper, and tape it up against the wall. With the burnt end of a stick she had prepared, we had to make a large "X" several times on the paper, chanting with each stroke "March! March! March! I'll get you before you get me!" She insisted that it was more effective if said in Italian. I guess something was probably lost in the translation.

Joseph M. Conforti

∞ Other Uses For Olive Oil ∞

Whenever a child in Grandma's family or a neighbor's child had a stomach ache, she would lie the child down, expose the child's stomach area and rub a blend of olive oil and minced garlic on the affected area. Within a few minutes the ache would usually disappear.

When family or close friends had a headache, grandma would sit the "patient" on a chair at her kitchen table, place a bowl of water before the person and add a drop of olive oil to the bowl. If the drop of olive oil formed an "eye," both the patient and grandma would recite a special prayer to remove the ache. Lo and behold, the headache would lessen or be gone in a few minutes.

Grandma was not a particularly superstitious person, however she believed in the "evil eye." She would often warn her children and grandchildren to beware when someone offered a compliment, such as "you are pretty " or "that's a nice new suit you have on," or "this cake you baked is delicious." Then it was time to place your thumb between your forefinger and middle finger and put your hand behind your back. This was to ward off the evil spirit in case an envious or jealous person related the compliment. This gesture was protection against the "evil eye."

William LoVerde

∞ Grandma's Ritual ∞

When I was about nine years old I was awakened one morning with severe pain in my face. My jaw was so swollen I didn't recognize myself in my bedroom mirror. I had so much discomfort that my mother suggested that I not attend school that morning.

She was so concerned about how I felt that she immediately phoned my grandmother Felice, who lived next door to explain my discomfort. Within a few minutes after my mother hung up the telephone, I heard our side door open and then heard Grandma tramping up the stairs to the second floor. I could hear her jingling from the moment she entered the house. She raced into my bedroom, breathless, and quickly but gently placed three or four religious medals in the area of the swelling on my face, while reciting several prayers in Italian. This went on for several minutes.

Later that morning, after making an appointment with our family dentist, my mother took me to his office. Upon examination, he discovered that I had two infected front teeth. After pumping my gums with Novocain, he drilled a drain hole in the problem area. Within a few minutes the pain had lessened substantially. By the time we arrived home the pain was completely gone.

That evening Grandma came to see how I was feeling. She was proud of the fact that her cure had worked. We did not tell her that it was the dentist and not her ritual that had rid me of my sore jaw.

Jacquelyn Felice Kelly

∞ General and Specific Healing Practices ∞

My uncle Luciano resided on the west side of Rochester, New York with his wife, Rosina, their five children and his teenage brother, Arturo. Late one hot summer night, we all were awakened by the crying of their four-year-old child, Orlando, who complained of severe stomach cramps and abdominal pain. Uncle Luciano and Aunt Rosina immediately put to use an old tried and true remedy – applying a poultice of grated zucchini squash to Orlando's abdomen. They summoned Arturo to go outside to the back yard garden to bring back a sizeable zucchini.

Arturo groped his way to the back yard with the aid of a dim lantern and managed to locate the patch of zucchini. On his return to the house, while carrying a large zucchini, he accidentally stumbled and fell into an open pit of human sewage over which, an outhouse once stood. Recently installed sanitary sewers made outhouses obsolete.

Arturo, soaked in sewage and stench managed to extricate himself from the pit and headed back to the house. The zucchini was washed immediately, grated and prepared for the poultice which was then applied to Orlando's abdomen. The focus of attention then switched to Arturo who stripped and bathed in a galvanized tub of hot water. His clothes were boiled in a copper boiler, then laundered.

Happily, within a day, Orlando's pains had subsided, Arturo's odorous clothing smelled clean, and the problem of the open pit had all been remedied.

On another occasion, I woke up with a painfully sore and stiff neck. My mother consulted a neighbor and they decided that my problem might be relieved by a visit to Donna Provedenza who had treated numerous individuals for all sorts of ailments, many who had, apparently, been victims of *mal 'occhio*, the evil eye, very likely inflicted on an innocent person by some jealous or ill-wishing onlooker.

So my mother carted off her seven year old son to see Donna Provedenza who lived five blocks away. Donna was an elderly, well built woman, with large and strong muscular arms and hands. She seated me and loosened my shirt and collar. After examining the area that hurt, she padded off to the kitchen and returned with a bowl containing a mixture of olive oil and vinegar and placed it on a table. Then she lit two six-inch long candles, placing them on either side of the bowl and began to recite prayers in Italian. She started anointing my forehead as well as the back of my head. She continued praying as she immersed both hands into the liquid mixture and proceeded to massage my neck vigorously. As the minutes lapsed and the prayers and massage continued, my neck felt warm then hot. Finally, she removed her hands, stopped praying, and wrapped and pinned a wide woolen cloth around my neck.

My mother thanked her with a monetary donation and we were told that if the pain and stiffness persisted beyond one or two days we should feel free to return for further spiritual and physical therapy.

In the 1930's we had a friend of the family named Betty. She was at home one afternoon when she decided to give a message to her father who was working on the roof of the house cleaning the gutters of debris. As she stepped outside, she was horrified to find her father lying on the ground next to the ladder. He was motionless, eyes open and his dentures had fallen from his mouth. Her frantic cries alerted the neighbors who called for an ambulance. He was in a coma for several days. Fortunately, he responded to treatment and returned to work after several days.

However, the experience had so traumatized Betty that she continued to remain depressed and in a daze most of the time. Betty's parents as well as several of her close relatives felt that her condition required spiritual therapy by none other than Donna Provedenza. After a serious of visits, prayers and repeated anointings, Betty's condition gradually returned to normal.

A crawling, vine-like, wild growing herb called *malva* in Italian, (botanically "mallow" in English), has been revered for years as an almost sacred healer by many Italians. For example, a wad of cooked malva could relieve a bad toothache. It could also rid the inflammation and discomfort of a canker sore. Furthermore, hot malva tea could soothe the symptoms of a cough or cold and was also regarded as a reliever of indigestion and stomach cramps.

For a number of years my father would journey into the fields during late fall to harvest several baskets of malva. He'd wash it then hang it outdoors to dry before storing it in a clean fabric sack for use during the following year.

Joseph M. Cappiello

∞ Remedies and Superstitions ∞

My grandmother was an interesting lady. She had remedies for many illnesses, mostly with herbs or with tea. My favorite was her remedy for an upset stomach. For adults it was bay leaf tea. For children it was sugar cubes in bay leaf tea. It worked all the time. We always had an upset stomach when we children visited her, because the tea tasted so good. Other remedies were not so pleasant.

The most vivid one in my memory was that of carefully placing a leech on a skin infection or a boil. It was a terrible feeling watching a tiny leech suck out bad blood. I wondered, at the time, how it felt. Ironically, I found out about fifteen years later in the jungles of Burma while with the Army Corps of Engineers in World War II. During the monsoon season, leeches would fall from the trees in the jungle and crawl inside our tents and into our uniforms. It was amazing how a tiny leech could grow to the size of your thumb from sucking out your blood.

My mother was no exception when it came to being a superstitious Italian. I think most Italian American families had that same mentality. At our dinner table each evening, when my mother folded one corner of the tablecloth over onto the table, it signaled, not only that dinner was over, but also that the Lord had just left.

Holy water had great significance in our lives. A small bottle of holy water was placed in every bedroom in our home to ward off evil spirits. It was also sprinkled in each room of a new home for the same reason and sprinkled in a new automobile for good luck – no expensive repairs, no bad accidents.

The evil eye, *mal 'occhio*, was greatly feared. When-ever anyone bought a new car, a new dress, a new suit, a new house, or received a promotion, or some good news, there was a fear that someone out there was either envious or had a malicious wish to harm. To avoid the maliciousness, attaching a small red ribbon on yourself or on your new purchase would prevent the "evil eye" from causing harm to you.

And to provide for a quick sale of your home, car, or any other large item, a small statue of Saint Joseph was placed upside down in your garden or front lawn. It remained there until the sale was complete.

Joseph Mileo

∞ La Gomare ∞

At the age of six, soon after he emigrated from the province of Calabria in Italy, my father lived in the Dyker Heights section of Brooklyn in a two-family house his parents shared with Zio Serafino's family.

"We did go to doctors when we were ill," he assured me. "But for most minor ailments and injuries we called upon *La Gomare*."

She was a woman about forty-five or fifty years old, not any more remarkable than his own mother or the rest of the immigrant women on the block. She possessed no medical degree, nor was she even a nurse, but either her know-how or some unknown magical abilities caused all the Italian families in the area to seek her services.

When persistent warts appeared on my father's hands, the woman dipped slices of raw potatoes into the black drippings of pressed eggplant and rubbed the potatoes over the warts. Within a few days the unsightly growths disappeared. One day, my father dislocated his ankle while playing football in the street. His mother called *La Gomare* who tugged and yanked at the twisted ankle until it slipped back into place. She then set the ankle with a pasty mixture of egg whites and gauze. It actually became a sort of cast when it dried. The following day, the gym teacher, Mr. Miller asked my father if he had seen a doctor.

"No," my father responded as though Mr. Miller should have known better. "*La Gomare* fixed it."

On occasion, *La Gomare* would mumble unintelligible words as she rubbed her fingers on my grandmother's forehead to cure a headache, or placed a string of garlic around my aunt's neck to repel the "evil eye" that brought her a fever. Mustard plasters almost always cured symptoms of the grippe.

But *La Gomare's* expertise was truly tested the day that Zio Serafino was advised by a medical doctor to restrict his intake of wine to one glass a day, in order to lower his blood pressure. Zio, who could always be found with a DiNobile cigar clenched between his teeth, consumed an average of four glasses of wine each day. Finding the Doctor's advise unbearable, Zio Serafino sought the counsel of *La Gomare*, who, unfortunately, agreed with the doctors orders.

"Ma ti posso aiutare," she said, assuring him that there was one thing that she could do for him. She left the room momentarily, then returned with a glass the size of a vase capable of holding a bouquet of sunflowers. She handed the large vase to Zio and said, *"Ecco!"*

Marisa Labozzetta

Immigrant Experiences

Remembering Pa

∞ Becoming Americans ∞

My grandparents never did fit into what I believed was American. I was often embarrassed by their mixture of Italian and English especially when they would "speaka likea thisa" to me while I was with my non-Italian American friends. And whenever we would do something wrong, they would yell to us, "Look at that 'merican!" as though being an American was something that shamed our family.

We finally became Americans when the Fazzolo family moved in next door. They were the new Italians, and even though our lives were separated only by a picket fence and a small garden that the previous owners had neglected for years, we were worlds apart. Until they moved in, whether or not we wanted it to be, we were America's Italians. In spite of the fact that our speech was only seasoned with the Italian that was the primary language of our grandparents and hamburgers and hot dogs had begun replacing lunches of "pasta e fagioli" or escarole and beans we were still the Italians, if only because others saw us as having different names, noses, or skin color. But this all changed the day the Fazzolo family moved in next door.

It was early spring when their moving van pulled up outside our home. I was playing outside, pretending not to notice them as they carried boxes and furniture from the street onto their front porch. My mother yelled for me to lend them a hand, and I pretended not to hear her. She came out of our house, grabbed me by the arm and dragged me over to where they had gathered to take a break. When my mother tried to speak to them in English, they could barely respond, and so Mr. Fazzolo asked if she spoke Italian. She tried, but she spoke a dialect that hadn't changed in over thirty years that made them snicker and scratch their heads. As though in some form of retaliation, I decided it was OK to laugh and mock their broken English. I helped them, only because my mother had forced me, and throughout the whole ordeal not a word passed between us.

These were the Italians who immigrated to America during the 1950s. We called them immigrants with wings, for they came to America in airplanes, unlike my grandparents, who had crossed the Atlantic in overcrowded boats. These people came with a truck load of possessions, not like my grandparents who were lucky if they could carry along a cardboard suitcase or a sack stuffed with what they had to bring to America. You would have thought that there would have been a natural affinity between the two groups of immigrants, but nothing could have been further from the truth. They came better educated and with a greater knowledge of America than had their turn-of-the-century predecessors.

They had been prepared by years of association with American soldiers, and the subsequent media invasion of their culture. They arrived more like Americans, yet they remained quite different. To us they were the new greaseballs, and we wouldn't let them forget it. It took a few years for the Fazzolos to become more like us, but in the process, we were becoming more like them. Mrs. Fazzolo would send over samples of her homemade cooking. My grandfather worked with Mr. Fazzolo to triple his yearly production of wine. My grandmother joined Mrs. Fazzolo in their backyard for the drying of tomatoes into paste. They rejuvenated my grandparents' Italian and kept the sound alive so that later, when I finally decided to study my ancestral language, my pronunciation would be near perfect.

Years later, after I had learned Italian, I went back to my old neighborhood and spoke, for the first time, at length with the people next door in what I had come to call "our language." I learned that Mr. Fazzolo had been a *partigiano* during World War II and had spent three months in a fascist prison until he was freed by Allied soldiers. He told me about having witnessed the machine gunning of innocent people by the Nazis; he told me how his father had been shot by a firing squad; he told me how his whole family had been driven out of their village for fear of their lives. And all that he told me made me ashamed of how we had first treated them when they moved into the house next door.

Essentially their immigration had created two types of Italian Americans. They maintained contact with Italy, and every few years took trips back. But as the years passed, and the trips grew fewer and farther between, the people next door eventually grew to be different from contemporary Italians so that if for some reason a new immigration to America had begun, our next door neighbors would be viewed by the new immigrants as American.

Fred L. Gardaphe

∞ The Dowry ∞

When World War I ended, Antonio and Mariantonia Conte eagerly awaited the return of their son Rocco who had served as a *Bersagliere* in some of the most ferocious battles of the war. He had been away for most of the war's duration. Besides their obvious feelings of anticipation to see him, they also wondered if he, like so many other returning veterans, would be seeking a wife with a substantial dowry. In addition to Rocco there were three unmarried daughters in the Conte household. And the war had left a shortage of eligible men. Those who did return to the village of Picerno in the Province of Potenza were at a premium and the going price of dowries was 10,000 Lire. The offers which matchmakers brought to Rocco, though substantial, were not enticing enough. Mother Mariantonia felt that because Rocco had "seen Paree" she would set in motion her plan for the family to immigrate to the United States.

Her husband was not anxious to leave Picerno. At the age of sixty-nine he was a pensioner who had worked as a timekeeper at the railroad station for many years. He was saddened to leave behind his older sons from a previous marriage even though they were married, had families of their own, and regarded Mariantonia as the only mother they had ever known. But Mariantonia was determined to see that Marta, Carmela, and Lucia espoused without having to spend 30,000 Lire on them in Picerno. Making heart-wrenching decisions was not new to Mariantonia. In 1904 and 1905 she had sent her young sons and daughters, Domenico, Adelaide, Nicola, and Rosina to America where they all married and had a brood of children. She missed not being part of those wedding celebrations and not being able to witness the birth of her twenty grandchildren. But those were small sacrifices compared to the larger one that she would be asking her family to make in order for them to be reunited after fifteen years.

It was April 1920 when they boarded a ship called the *Madonna* in Naples bound for America. Their only tangible reminders of home were the latest posed photos they had taken with the relatives and friends they were to leave behind. All other property had been sold in order to afford the cost of passage. Conditions aboard the ship were quite tolerable except for the turbulent weather which prevailed for almost all of the three weeks it took for them to arrive at Ellis Island, where Domenico and

Nicola awaited them.

Before immigration processing began, passengers were treated to a substantial lunch. Antonio was puzzled, however, when a beverage he had mistaken for moscato wine, upon tasting, turned out to be tea. "Tea is for sick people. What kind of country doesn't drink wine at midday?" he remarked. The entire family passed their physicals except for Lucia who had developed a rash. The rash was deemed suspicious by the examiner so with white chalk he scribbled a large "X" on her jacket lapel and isolated her from the group. He took her to an area for those who might possibly be quarantined. Those years in the trenches had taught Rocco to react quickly and without hesitation he erased the "X," grabbed Lucia by the arm and whisked her toward the exit door. At this point, her wicker basket flew open sending four provoloni cascading down the stairs. He told her not to pick them up. She ignored him and scooped them up on their way down the stairs. While crying she told Rocco that after three weeks of caring for the provoloni she had no intention of leaving them behind. The Italian cheese was her gift for the relatives. On the way to their temporary lodgings in the Bronx, Lucia's rash mysteriously disappeared as quickly as it did had appeared; she was not a carrier of some new plague.

Three days later, dressed in their new American clothes, Marta, Carmela, and Lucia were riding the Third Avenue elevated train, to their first day of employment in the garment district. After three months with all four young people working, the family settled into a three-bedroom apartment in Italian Harlem. They had purchased all the furnishings from an immigrant family who were returning to Poland after having made their fortune.

As Mariantonia had reasoned, it wasn't long before suitors were beating a path to their door, and on this side of the ocean, it was they who brought offerings. Marta, as her mother and grandmother before her, married a widower. He was Neopolitan with a steady job with the New York City transit system. He had a fully furnished apartment in the Bronx and a motorcycle with a sidecar for her to ride in with his young son. Carmela wound up in New Jersey with a Sicilian husband who had just completed a three-bedroom house. He maintained a stable of horses, which he used in his successful recycling business.

At twenty years of age, Lucia had already turned down a jeweler with a shop of his own as well as a tailor from Maddaloni, her father's birthplace.   She respected the former for his entrepreneurial expertise, but she could sense that his life would be too involved in his business. The latter, though charming, thought little of punctuating his conversation with "off color" phrases which were so common in the Neopolitan vernacular. To her, this seemed so undignified and crass. Mariantonia agreed that money wasn't everything and that Lucia should hold out for something better.

One night, while her father and brother were playing cards at the local men's club, Michele Buccino got a glimpse of Lucia as she waited in the entrance of the card room. He fell in love at first sight. Sensing that no respectable woman would ever enter a room filled with hard-drinking card-playing men, Michele went over to introduce himself, offering her a glass of wine. She politely refused. She never drank wine but asked him to remind her father and brother that dinner awaited them at home. As he left to relay her message, he noted her fair completion and beautiful auburn colored hair.

Several days later Michele asked Mariantonia's permission to court Lucia. As a self-supporting teenager he had left his family in Italy, traveling to Argentina where he lived until the outbreak of the war. Although stricken with malaria during this conflict, he had proven to be so courageous that fifty years later the Italian government conferred on him the title of Cavaliere, while awarding him a medal of honor for bravery, as well as a pension. After the war, he continued his occupation as a master cabinetmaker.

His proposal of marriage to Lucia was accompanied by a diamond engagement ring. Lucia sewed and embroidered her trousseau of bed linens, tablecloths, nightgowns, and crocheted nightcaps. He too worked hard creating all the furniture required of their first apartment.

With three daughters well married, Antonio and Mariantonia had finally accomplished what they knew would not have happened in such a short time, if ever, in Italy. So they looked to Rocco who had successfully made the transition into the working world as an agent selling insurance to the Italian community. He enjoyed his single status so much that his bachelorhood lasted for seventeen years after setting foot on U.S. soil. It was quite awhile after his sisters married that he proposed to Adelina. Because she was a divorcee, their marriage could not be sanctioned by the church, yet Mariantonia gave them her blessing sensing that Adelina would make him a good wife along with her two children who adored Rocco.

The saga of how and why the Conte family emigrated was usually related in much greater detail as we were growing up, by my parents Lucia and Michele Buccino. They were married for fifty-three years. Antonio's pocket watch and Mariantonia's pendant and earrings set, Lucia's engagement ring, and Michele's handmade furniture are just a few of the possessions which we inherited. But the most precious legacy of all were the reminiscences and memories they so often imparted to their children and grandchildren.

Teresa Cerasuola

∞ La Famiglia ∞

My grandmother, Angelina Felice, came to America from Italy as young married woman and settled in Geneva, New York. She gave birth to nine children and was an inspiration to the entire family, especially after her husband, my grandfather, died from a work-related accident. Her oldest child was married with two young children at the time. All thirteen people lived in the same tiny house at 26 North Street. I can't imagine where they all slept.

One day, fifty-three year old grandpa went to work and did not return. He allowed my father, who was seventeen at the time, to tag along with him that day. Grandpa was buried alive while digging for a sewage disposal plant at the Willard State Hospital. My father was witness to grandpa's death as workers attempted, in vain, to raise him out of the ground.

As the youngest boy, my father always took special care of his mother, as he still cares for his wife and daughter. He is a veteran of World War II and frequently sent money home to his wife and mother that he had saved from his army paychecks. I was a small child when he returned from the War. Upon returning, he ordered plans for what was known as a "pre-built home" and erected a new house for his immediate family. When he completed it, he built one for his mother and two more for other sisters. The houses were built in close proximity to each other. The youngest sister still lives in one of them. All told, he built five houses in Geneva in his spare time. His full time employment was that of a civilian administrator at the Seneca Ordinance Depot. He never spoke of the secret government environment at the Depot or the kind of items that were stored there. He retired in 1971.

My mother's parents also came from Italy. They had eleven children. At present my mother is in her mid eighties and has three older sisters. The oldest is one hundred and one. Mother's father started the Monaco Grocery, a store on Washington Street in Geneva while working full time at another job. His children managed the store until he was able to handle it full time. The Monaco family was a little "better off" than the Felice family and I'm not sure that they really relished the fact that one of their daughters, my mother, hooked up with a guy from "the other end of town."

Catholic parishes geographically divided Geneva. Saint Francis church was located at the "butt end" of town where the poorer folks lived. The "well off" people lived at Saint Stephen's part of town. In spite of this "class" issue, we all got along pretty well. It was customary for girls to marry an Italian from their "end" of town. It was an exception if one married a non-Italian. At times, I felt that the whole population of the city were my relatives. Imagine my growing up with eighteen aunts and uncles, not to mention countless number of cousins.

Jacquelyn Felice Kelly

∞ My Mother Was One of Them ∞

On November 8, 2000, President Clinton signed into law a bill that confirmed the deprivation of civil rights that befell Italian American aliens at the outset of World War II. For some six hundred thousand Italian (subjects) immigrants it meant severe restrictions on travel, types of employment, use of cameras and radios, etc.

This was an experience that struck my own household because my mother was one of them. She had arrived from Sicily with my father in 1927, and like many of her co-nationals had not yet obtained United States citizenship because of preoccupation with raising a family, unemployment, and poverty during the Great Depression. In addition, she had the hardship of being a single parent after my father's death in 1938. The struggle for survival left little time to concern herself with political matters. In this regard, she was no different from many in my neighborhood who depended on assistance from government and private agencies as well as from kindly disposed relatives, to make ends meet.

With a suddenness that followed the declaration of war on December 8, 1941, our family had to adjust to my mother being labeled an "enemy alien." Sixty years later, I can still recall myself as a thirteen-year-old boy being asked to take our short wave radio to the local radio repair shop to disconnect the short wave feature that was forbidden to enemy aliens and their households. It did not matter that my sister, brother and I were all natural born citizens – we were all affected and imposed upon because my mother was – an enemy alien. But the inconvenience of not having a short wave radio was minor compared to the unambiguous inference that our household was, somehow, less than American.

It did not matter that my siblings and I enthusiastically supported the war effort. It did not matter that we bought twenty-five cent stamps toward the purchase of War Bonds. It did not matter that we celebrated Allied victories on the battlefield. None of this mattered – my mother was one of them.

Fortunately, my mother did go to night school and obtained her citizenship paper during the course of the war. Nevertheless, now after so many years, I still cannot think about the event without tears and anger engulfing me over the humiliation that we endured. That testing time was not a happy one, and only with time did it recede into memories. However, the scars persist.

Salvatore J. LaGumina

∞ Guardian Angel ∞

I was five years old when the twins were born. In the middle of a June night, Papa rushed out of our small two-bedroom flat in East Harlem and returned with a short stout woman who ordered my father about with her sharp Italian tongue. When my older brother, sister, and I peered over the foot board of our bed into the kitchen, we saw the table covered with a blanket. A large blue and white basin had been placed on one of the two chairs that faced each other. Moments after my mother cried out, the stranger carried a tiny form and laid it on the table. She went back into the bedroom and, to our amazement, returned with yet another baby.

"There's two of them!" my brother cried. She proceeded to wash the babies and brought them back to my mother. Since the *levatrice*, or midwife, was usually paid five dollars if the new born was a girl and ten dollars for a boy, the delivery had been costly; fifteen dollars that my parents could barely afford.

Each twin weighed over eight pounds, which left my mother weakened and plagued with constant lower back pains. After a few days of help provided by my aunt, Mamma was once again submerged in her daily chores of cooking, cleaning house, and caring for the twin's needs. Grocery shopping was the most difficult chore, however, since she had to carry both Dorotea and Francesco down three flights of stairs, and settle them in the large straw twin carriage that was kept in the ground floor hallway. Then upon return, she had to carry the babies and groceries back up the three flights. She did this almost daily because our small icebox only kept one day's supply of fresh food.

To assure that the legs of each twin would grow with straight, strong leg bones and to prevent bowleggedness, Mamma wrapped both legs in a tight bandage with a long swaddling cloth band called *una fascia*. Because tenement children were deprived of sunshine, the lack of vitamin D caused rickets, and to immigrants the *fascia* seemed to be the only solution.

When Mamma heard about the Board of Health opening a new clinic on 123rd Street, only two blocks away, she brought the babies over there for a checkup. The clinic was operated by the city and provided three nurses to administer to poor immigrant families. The fee was twenty-five cents per visit. It was located on the ground floor of an ordinary tenement whose inside walls had been removed and the remaining structure painted white. The antiseptic cleanliness of the room impressed me, but more so, the good Samaritans who worked there. Mamma promised the nurses that she would visit regularly to have the twins weighed and examined. But fate was to deal my parents a shattering blow before the passing of a year's time.

In March 1929 when Frankie was nine months old, his

breathing suddenly became very difficult. His appetite was poor. He had been the sturdy one of the two, who, after finishing his bottle, would reach over and snatch Dorotea's bottle to drink, as well. Believing that he had a cold, Mamma rubbed his chest with Vicks and covered it with a warmed woolen cloth to loosen the phlegm. Two days later the baby's condition worsened and a strange sound came from his throat. Mamma quickly wrapped him in a blanket and brought him to the corner druggist, Mr. Grillo, asking for some medication. One look at the baby made Mr. Grillo urge my mother to take him to a doctor right away. Mamma took the baby to the only doctor she knew, Dr. Costanza, on 116th Street. An obese man, who lacked a gentle bedside manner, he angrily threw down his stethoscope after examining Frankie and raised his hands in futility.

"It's too late. Why didn't you bring him to see me sooner?" he yelled. "The baby will live for only a few more hours. He has diphtheria."

Mamma was shocked. She carried Frankie home, placed him on her bed and waited for Papa to come home from work to tell him the devastating news. We children were sent to our next door neighbor's house, but after eating very little of the food that was served, I silently slipped away and returned to our flat. I quietly went into my darkened bedroom and remained there, watching my parents in their lighted bedroom at the other end of the house. There was a macabre silence as the angel of death hovered over the little form on the bed. Then I heard a strange gurgling sound emanate from the baby's lungs. Mamma screamed his name and Papa uttered a loud mournful groan as they both fell to their knees beside the bed. Their son Francesco was dead just four hours after Mamma had left Dr. Costanza's office.

Frankie's wake was held in the kitchen. The table upon which the twins had been placed at birth was removed. In its place stood a white coffin atop a bier. Candles set in ruby colored glasses on tall brass candle holders along side of the casket cast a crimson glow. All about the room were sprays of flowers sent from friends and relatives. I tried to tell myself that my little brother was merely sleeping and would soon be awake to prove that he was not really dead.

On the morning of the funeral, I waited on the front stoop until the white hearse arrived along with the four hired automobiles that would transport mourners to the cemetery. When we were told that children were not allowed to go to the cemetery, I started crying and insisted that I had a right to go because Frankie had been my brother. Papa's *paesano*, Pasquale Grigone, came to my rescue. He told the family that I should be allowed to go and that I could ride in the same car with his family. He gently lifted me into the last car in the procession.

As the little white casket was lowered into the ground, my mother cried with arms outstretched, as if trying to reclaim her son. She let out a wail and collapsed into my father's arms. After a series of prayers were recited, I gently laid a flower onto the casket as a final good bye to Frankie. Other mourners paid their last respects in the same manner.

After a short time, Mamma seemed to resume her household duties in a very normal manner. Frankie was not mentioned. Then one day when she and I were alone in the house, she went into her bedroom and pulled out a large metal trunk that contained her valuables. She lifted the lid and withdrew a gold inkwell shaped like a crab that had been a wedding gift, and the silk handkerchief her brother had sent her from France during World War I, with "To My Dear Sister" embroidered on it. She also removed a small gold watch that Papa had given her when they were married. I waited for her to bring out these treasures so that I could see them once again but, instead, she lifted a little white satin romper from the trunk that Frankie had worn for his christening. She clasped it to her heart and cried out his name.

Not wanting me to see her like this, she ran into the bathroom still clutching the romper. There her grief exploded into loud sobs. She was sitting on the closed toilet seat, swaying back and forth with the romper still pressed to her breast when I entered the bathroom to comfort her. I placed my hand on her arm.

"Mamma, you musn't cry because Frankie is now a little angel in heaven, and we are lucky to have him watching over us."

She stopped crying, and dropped the romper into her lap. She took me in her arms, squeezed me tightly and I knew that Mamma would never let *me* go.

Viola Medori Labozzetta

∞ Pa Lost Them All ∞

My father came to America in the early 1900's and settled in Pennsylvania where he labored very hard in the coal mines. Later he moved to Rochester, New York where he was married to my mother. His employment in Rochester was in a saw mill. In those days there were no safe guards on machines, no compensation laws from which to draw monetary or medical benefits, so when he lost a finger on one hand in a saw mill accident he was given a maintenance job at the mill for a few weeks, then he was laid off.

Fortunately, he saved most of his earnings while working in the coal mines so during the period from the early 1920's to 1930 he began purchasing single and two family homes on Rochester's west side. He bought two houses on Maple Street, one on Jay Street and one on York Street during an eight year period. Houses, at that time, could be purchased for between five-hundred and seven-hundred dollars. One of the houses on Maple Street was a two family home. Pa thought these rental properties would sustain his family which eventually grew to ten children. His other thought was that when his children married, they would each have a place of their own, to live. In the interim, the rent he received from these properties allowed our family a modest lifestyle. The stock market crash of 1929 meant that Pa's renters were not able to pay their monthly rent and, therefore, Pa was not able to pay the real estate and school taxes when due.

One by one, the City foreclosed on each of Pa's properties. For each of the foreclosures Pa was paid the sum of one-dollar at the closing. Pa lost them all.

Vincent Fazio

∞ Dreams of America ∞

The sky was blue and cloudless the day
the gingham dresses came, the light
unfettered by screens filling the window,
my mother opening the cloth-wrapped box
eager for what news these messengers brought
from that other world. And as they emerged from
their white cocoons, creased, stiff with sizing,
she held them up to the light, marveled
at the bright improbable colors,
wondering aloud: "Are these meant for me,
have they forgotten what it's like here?"
amazed they would think she could wear
peach and white, white and apple-green,
yet holding each dress in turn against her -
square neckline, sleeves like budding wings -
lost in the mirror, trying on as well,
maybe, the life that went with them.
In the dream I dream for her, the one
who stayed behind, she stands on the porch
of a brick house, like the one her father
would buy on Belasco Avenue, with a yard
and small rounded bushes, or walks alone
and anonymous in the crowd of a city street.
She doesn't lower her eyes, and she smiles,
whenever she feels like it, no longer afraid
of compromising herself, of the unleashing the
evil eye.

Rina Ferrarelli

∞The Home of the Brave and the Free ∞

Shrubs and trees dominate the rocky land;
On grassy hills the grazing gray sheep stand.
In ancient times, Marrucini and Frentini presided here;
In recent times, Michetti and Galiani resided near.

Our peasants' huts are low, one roomed hovels,
With floors of lyed earth or of brown stone.
A farmer digs with a plow, and he grovels,
To grow grapes on land he does not own.

We share our home with some chickens and pigs.
The men walk several miles to the field,
Return home for a meal of bread, cheese and figs,
Which women make from their small farm's yield.

My body aches; my mind is weary;
My spirit is mad, sad and dreary.
To America – a land of honey, milk and gold,
To America – a place of money, and stone cold.

Buildings and billboards dominate the land,
On concrete paths the milling shoppers stand.
In ancient times, Oneidas and Mohawks presided here.
In recent times, Van Buren and Roosevelt resided near.

My two brothers and I live in a teeming tenement;
Our bedroom window overlooks the crowded street.
Muscled men move the dark earth with shovels and the
intent
Of building subways beneath the rambling feet.

We share our home with some roaches and mice;
I travel three long miles to work the site.
For lunch, we dole out bread, cheeses and rice,
Which I eat with delight, to the last bite.

I long to return to the land of my birth,
And work once again with my hands in the earth.
I feel great despair and sorrow,
But things may improve tomorrow.

For generations the Belfiglio family lived in virtual poverty as peasant farmers, *contadini*, in the village of Roccamontepiano in the harsh climate and rugged mountains of Abruzzo, Italy. They toiled with crude tools to grow crops, tended vineyards, and herded sheep on land they did not own. They lived in a small shelter. Only close family ties and their Catholic faith sustained them. Most staples were made at home or grown in their small garden.

One day the father, Antonio, felt the need to hold a family conference. His stern brown eyes, beneath graying dark hair, displayed sadness; but his voice was resolute. He told his wife Lucia and the eight children that their meager family income could not support all of them. Lucia said nothing, but her eyes welled with tears. Her three unmarried sons, Valentino, Carlo, and Liberto would migrate to America.

In 1902 the brothers traveled overland with donkeys laden with baskets and bundles to the railroad station at Sulmona. They had thirty-four dollars among them. They travelled by train to Naples where they boarded a ship whose rough crossing lasted sixteen days. The three were among the two thousand passengers jammed into steerage class. Their berths were two feet wide and six feet in length;

two and one half feet between bunks. Passengers ate their meals and slept in these areas. The stench of body odor and vomit was hard to bear.

Finally, a moment of joy arrived; the sight of the Statue of Liberty from the deck of the ship stirred varied emotions. Some passengers displayed theirs outwardly, others in silence. None, however, could see the inscription on the inside of the pedestal of the one hundred and fifty-two foot steel-reinforced copper female figure: "Give me your tired, your poor, your huddled masses yearning to breathe free."

Officials herded immigrants into stalls for processing at Ellis Island. Economic uncertainty and culture shock were threatening realities. Weeks after passing through the Island the three brothers found backbreaking work, using crude tools to help build the New York City subway system. They had replaced the exhausting farm labor of Italy for the exhausting city labor of America.

They were strangers in a strange land. They spoke no English and several social groups rejected them. In their dilapidated one-room apartment they wrote letters to their loved ones in Abruzzo. They had known anguish, poverty, and misery in Italy. They added loneliness to these in New York.

Membership in a new organization, the Sons of Italy, provided them with the support and opportunities for friendship, respect, personal value, and mutual aid. Somehow through perseverance they endured and eventually prospered through hard work, frugality, an iron will, and the willingness to adapt.

Valentine J. Belfiglio

∞ Divestiture ∞

She unpinned the folds
of white linen
eloquent of place,
loosened the loops
and braided knots,
and combed her hair
into a bun.
She untied her apron,
took off one by one
the pleated skirts,
the black jacket
with wide velvet cuffs,
the padded camisole,
the long shirt
articulate with lace.
Then stepped into a dress
skimpier than a slip,
and naked,
exposed like that,
my grandmother
came to America.

Rina Ferrarelli

∞ Remembering Pa ∞

Pa came to the United States from Italy in 1907 at the age of fifteen. He settled on the West Side directly behind the Rochester, New York General Hospital, which was located on West Main Street. After marrying, he opened a grocery store on Prospect Street, adjacent to the hospital.

For the hospital's maternity ward expansion project in 1930, the City needed to purchase several properties in the immediate area of the hospital including Pa's grocery store, as well as our residence. He didn't like the idea of having to sell this property after all the hard work it took to purchase the dwelling and to start a business. This was his family's livelihood, his sole source of income. Another factor was that he was given a much lower price for the property than he would have received under different circumstances. Interestingly, during the 1950 s, two of his three children, Barbara and Thomas were born in the new maternity ward at the Rochester General Hospital on the exact property where I was born in 1926. What a thrilling coincidence!

Pa did not remain without work for very long. After the demolition of the store he became a self employed cabinetmaker, paperhanger, house renovator, and house painter, skills he learned as a young man in Italy. At times he would utilize his sons to assist him in the various work projects in which he was involved. Pa negotiated the cost of each project, which was usually at an hourly rate.

For a specific exterior painting job of a three story multiple family dwelling, in the mid to late 1930's, Pa required the help of three of his sons; Louis was painting at the third story level, Joseph at the second story, and Pa at the first level. Because I was the youngest, at age ten, I was the runner, gathering tools, paint , brushes, drop cloths, etc.

During the second day of painting, my brother Louis was curious as to how much each of us was being paid for our labor. He yelled down from the third story of the house,

"Pa, how much are we being paid for our work?"

"Fifty cents an hour," Pa replied.

"That's pretty good pay, Pa, fifty cents for you, fifty cents for me, fifty cents for Joseph, and fifty cents for Vincent."

"No, no, Louis, fifty cents an hour, not for each of us, only for me!"

Frustrated, Louis quickly climbed down the ladder, threw his paint brush to the ground and vehemently exclaimed, "Pa, I quit."

Vincent Natale

∞ Ellis Island ∞

Enduring
listening
learning ---
immigrants
smiled,
interim
silent
languages
alphabetizing
new
dreams

Sal Parlato, Jr.

Snapshots

Reflections

∞ Playing It Cool ∞

My father made bootleg alcohol. He sold quantities of this wonderful "white lightning" to his close friends and associates. During the late 30's, 40's and early 50's, it was customary for Italian immigrants to make cordials for holiday consumption. The most popular cordials of that era were anisette and creme de menthe (both white and green), although several other flavors were produced as well. One could always find homemade cordials at Italian weddings made by the bride and groom's parents. These drinks were served at every wedding I attended during this period.

When Pa made deliveries of alcohol, which were usually scattered throughout various neighborhoods of Rochester, New York, he would drive his pickup truck into the detached garage behind our house, close the garage door, and carefully load the one and five gallon cans of alcohol onto the back of the truck. Then he would yell for us kids who were usually playing in the street with friends. My two brothers and I would come running because we knew by the sound of Pa's voice that what he wanted us for was relatively important.

He would load us into the back of the truck directly behind the cab along with a couple of our friends, and ask us sit up straight so that we could be seen. Then he covered the cans of "hooch" with a large canvas. Everything looked so innocent. He figured that he would never be stopped by a policeman, not with three or four kids riding in the back of his truck. And he never was caught.

Edward Gala

∞ Buying Chickens ∞

When I was a young girl my parents operated a small corner store in an Italian American, West Side neighborhood in Rochester, New York. I say "Italian American" because if you were not "Italian," that is, raised by parents who were born in Italy, then you were "American." It didn't matter if your parents were German, Irish, Polish, French, etc.; you were "American." The same was true for bread. If you were not eating Italian bread, it was obviously, "American" bread.

My father Mike was the proprietor of the store and knew all of his customers very well including Maria who was a very frugal person; no..., to be more precise, she was "tight," "cheap," and a wee bit of a drunk. When she had a little cash, she would shop elsewhere in the neighborhood for her groceries, her meats, cheese, vegetables, staples, etc. But when short on cash she would shop at my father's store, because he would always give her a "slip" (an IOU).

My father sold live chickens every Friday and Saturday at the store. He would drive to the farmer's market on Union Street each weekend morning at five o'clock to purchase all the products that he thought he would be able to sell in his market. These included chickens that were housed in wooden crates with round wooden bars, which afforded the chickens plenty of air, and a gated hinged opening on top. He usually came back from the market with two crates filled with chickens to start the weekend.

By the time he returned to his store, usually by eight o'clock, Maria would be there waiting to buy one or two chickens. For some reason the chickens always knew when Maria was close at hand because they would begin to flutter and cackle soon after her arrival. Her weekly ritual included opening the latch on top of each crate, grasping a chicken by the lower legs with her left hand. Her right hand, with middle finger extended, would be inserted into the chicken's rump to feel for an egg. This performance usually repeated itself several times before Maria was successful in achieving her goal. Of course, the chicken(s) with the egg(s) was the one(s) she purchased, with the bill "to be paid later."

Frances Romagnolo Gala

∞ Mamma's Return ∞

When I was a preteen, my father would sing his favorite Neopolitan classics. On some occasions I would join him, to our mutual delight. As an adult, I would recall these beautiful moments, but at the same time, I was bothered by the memory of my mother just listening and not singing along. I would wonder what was in my mother's mind during these moments. Was she happy to hear us sing or, was she being just the dutiful wife and mother. You see my father's voice was passable but mine is bad, really bad.

In the 1980's my mother was in the early stages of Alzheimer's, and by March 1992 she was placed in a nursing home. By 1993, when I was sixty-five years old, she had seriously deteriorated. As is typical with people who have this disease, she walked bent over, always looking at her feet, glassy eyed, mumbling incoherently, and not recognizing anyone.

One evening I went to visit her and we took our usual walk. We were strolling together slowly, mother bent over, looking at her feet, and mumbling. But, on this visit, I understood one word, "Gabriele." That was my father's name. Apparently she thought I was her husband. At some point she stopped 'talking.' After a while I thought, "If she thinks that I am Gabriele, why not sing a few of Gabriele's favorite songs?" I only sang a few notes when she suddenly looked at me with a stern stare and in a clear voice bellowed, "Shut up John." Just as quickly, she returned to her previous position. Somehow, she had recognized my voice and for a brief moment she was her old self again. And I found out what she had been thinking when she heard my father and me singing fifty years ago.

Some might think that I was devastated to learn that I had a voice "even a mother could not love." I was not. For a brief moment I had my mother back and that was a very precious moment.

John J. DeMatteo

∞ The Shoemaker ∞

One of my earliest childhood recollections involved an informal language class led by my father. He entered the United States at age seventeen to join his father. They were both skilled shoemakers in Italy and easily found work in one of the shoe manufacturing plants in Rochester, New York. When my father was drafted into the U. S. Army during World War I, this afforded him the opportunity to become fluent in the English language. After the war he continued his trade of shoe repair in several locations.

Finally, in 1927 his family settled in the house where I was born. The house included an attached storefront and was located at the corner of Orange and Grape streets. This is where I attended my informal language classes. Here is where I learned to speak Italian and several Italian immigrants learned to read and speak English.

The Great Depression of the 1930's left many men without jobs so several of them tended to congregate in my father's shoe shop. Most of them could not read or write other than their native language. Each day, my father would read and translate the English and Italian daily newspapers for them. As they learned the English language, they found that literacy meant that more jobs became available to them.

I became part of this daily routine and to this day, I rely on my second language to communicate with many of my patients who migrated to Rochester after World War II to work in the area's clothing factories. It was a wonderful experience that has benefited me all my life.

Charles H. Marino

∞ How They Met ∞

During the African Campaign of World War II, an Italian soldier, Adolfo Poletti, was captured by allied forces in Tunisia, (North Africa) and sent to a prisoner of war camp in the United States. He was first detained in Cheyenne, Wyoming then relocated to Denver, Colorado and finally sent to the Seneca Army Depot in Romulus, New York. During his detainment at the Seneca Army Depot, Italy became an ally to the U.S. forces. After this point in time a few extra privileges were granted to the prisoners. They were able to form teams and play soccer games and other sports. They also enjoyed dances held on the premises, to which the general public was invited.

Josephine D'Accursio, a resident of Fairport, New York, enjoyed going to dances at the camp along with her friends.

On a particular evening, she spotted Adolfo across the dance floor and, at once, announced to her friends that she was going to marry him. Their first dance was to the song, "Rum & Coca-Cola" by the Andrew Sisters. Over time she attended the dances often and enjoyed this blossoming relationship with him.

Josephine could not tell her very strict mother that she was seeing Adolfo, so when she wanted to go to the camp to visit him, she would say she was going to a friend's birthday party. Her plan was unique. She would send herself a birthday invitation to an imaginary party, and on the day of the party, she would wrap an empty box and leave the house under her mother's watchful eye. Soon after leaving the house she would throw the "birthday gift" in the Erie Canal, which she needed to cross on the way to catch the bus to Romulus.

The relationship was interrupted at the end of the war because Adolfo was sent back to Italy. They corresponded frequently and shortly after the war, Josephine gained passage on a Liberty ship and sailed for two weeks to reunite with Adolfo. Through the efforts of Adolfo's sisters, Lina and Maria, they were granted permission to get married at Saint Anne's Chapel, within the Vatican.

They returned to Fairport where they raised three daughters and one son. Adolfo passed away one month before their fortieth wedding anniversary.

Becoming an American citizen was very important to Adolfo. He was proud to be an Italian American. An annual award is presented to an eighth grade, male and female student, who has shown exemplary citizenship throughout their middle school years at the school where Aldolfo worked. This award is known as the "Adolfo Poletti Citizenship Award."

David Poletti

∞ Social Security ∞

My mother and father did not have a lot of money when I was growing up on the West Side of Rochester, New York. In fact they took in borders at their home to help pay the bills. They had nine children and realistically believed that during the depression they would never be able to afford a funeral for any of their children should that tragic event occur. So my parents obtained life insurance policies from the Prudential Insurance Company for each of us. The value of each policy was five hundred dollars, payable upon death. The insurance man came to our home each week and ma presented him with the nine payment books. He would enter into his ledger the five cents for each of the nine policies that Ma paid him for, add the date and his initials (years later the cost for each policy rose to ten cents a week).

This event occurred every week until each of ma and pa's chilcren were married. Then each child was responsible for continuing the policy, if they wished. A few years ago, more than seventy years after my parents purchased the policy for me, I received a phone call from Prudential because they were trying to locate policy holders from many years ago.

They indicated to me that the insurance policy for me was still in effect and wanted to know what did I intend to do regarding that fact. I was amazed to learn that the policy was worth ten times its original value.

Joe Boccacino

∞ Reflections ∞

During World War II we had five stars in our front window on Jay Street on the west side of Rochester, New York. Our neighbors, the D'Amato family had five and the Fedeles' on Wilder Street had eight stars. These stars indicated how many family members were in military service of our country. In addition, I had three more brothers in service during the Korean War. From 1941-1946, the population in my neighborhood was devoid of males of conscription age. Our mothers and fathers were in constant fear for the safety of their loved ones. They were pleased that all family members in the military returned safely from various theaters of Allied operations.

When I was in the seventh grade at Eli Whitney School #17, I was a pretty good student and I earned a Bronze Medal from the Sons of the American Revolution for scholarship, citizenship and leadership. The award was to be presented at a special ceremony at the school, and one or more parent of the awardees was required to attend. When I arrived home from school that afternoon, I ran in the front door of house and yelled, "Ma, ma you have to come to school because ... " That's as far as I got. I didn't have a chance to finish my sentence before Ma gave me a couple of whacks across the head and a few choice words along with them. She had assumed that I was causing trouble at school. After attending the award ceremony at the school on the scheduled date, she was proud that her son had been a good boy -- as she expected him to be.

My father had a large vegetable garden when we lived on Orange Street. The Pastor of our church, Father Joseph

Cirrincone, stopped by the house one day to ask my father why he didn't attend mass on Sundays. Pa remarked,
"I make sure that all my children attend. Besides, what sins can an old man like me commit? I don't even blaspheme." Of course, Father Joe went back to the rectory with an armful of fresh vegetables from my Pa's garden.

Vincent Fazio

∞ Personal Remembrances of World War II ∞

My father worked for the Baltimore and Ohio Railroad so as a family we moved every few years as his position with the railroad required. Therefore, I have remembrances of World War II from Chicago, Brooklyn, and Manhattan. When we lived in Chicago, dad was prepared to join the Unites States Marine Corps, but the B&O and the government felt that dad was in an essential job. So my mom did not give up our little apartment, find a job, or ask my grandparents to become babysitters.

The windows of our apartment had to be covered with blackout shades at night since it was believed that enemy bombers could navigate to their targets using the lights of the cities. Nonno Nascenzo DiDominico was an air raid warden for our block and one night brought us news that if the air raid practice had been real, our whole block would have been destroyed. This was a very sobering thought for a five-year old. I thought that those little falling parachutes would have made cute toys.

I often waited in line at our local public school for our ration books. I still have several of these little books in a treasured scrapbook. Toward the end of the War my dad was transferred to the New York City area. We lived in in Brooklyn where my memories were mostly happy ones.

One day we learned that a troop ship would be returning from Europe so mom took us down to the docks in Manhattan to see the arrival of the first one. I recall being in awe while looking up at that gigantic ship with all those returning servicemen. Each deck was completely covered with servicemen and they were even hanging from every porthole

Nonna Elizabeth DiDomenico and my mother were faithful about sending care packages to their relatives in Italy (Abruzzo). My soft-spoken mid-western mother found it very difficult dealing with personnel at our local Brooklyn Post Office. Every time she brought a package to be mailed to Italy, they seemed to change the packaging requirements. The clerks were often unpleasant in the manner they spoke to my mother. One day she had had it. She made ready to do battle with the Post Office. In her sternest tone, she told them just to tell her what she was required to do and she would do it. She never had any problems after that incident.

Diane Francesconi Lyon

∞ I Am From ∞

I am from a neat and clean house
Spotless bedrooms and
Family talks around the dinner table

I am from home made Italian dinners
Oil and Vinegar salad gets passed around first
Then comes the bread, fresh out of the oven

I am from fun filled weekends with family and friends
Whether it be a game of "Ghost in the Graveyard"
At the local cemetery at dusk,
Or afternoons on the lake

I am from going out to dinner with close relations
I am from the clinking of Crystal glasses and
Fancy sterling silverware of elegant restaurants
To neighborhood burger joints
And gooey ice cream cones with friends from
forever

I am from almost silent whispers at night
They kiss my ear and leave the words
"Good Night" ringing inside
I am from deafening shouts of "I Love You"
And silent looks that say the same

I am from the dolls and toys that shaped my
imagination and
Old photo albums stuffed with pictures,
Frozen moments that are now only distant
memories

Memories of smiles and frowns
Laughter and tears
Memories of where I am from

Tara Jackson

∞ Recollections of Grandma and Grandpa ∞

Grandma Sara and grandpa Frank LoVerde emigrated from Valedolmo, Sicily in the early 1900's. They produced six children, five boys and a girl. Grandpa's first employment was that of a construction worker on a spur of the Erie Canal. The family lived on the west side of Rochester, New York, specifically at 580 Oak Street. He later worked at the Gioia Macaroni Company, a couple of blocks from his home. Grandma was a housewife and a midwife. She delivered babies for Dr. Scinta.

The family had a garden and a shed for a goat that they kept and milked because one of their children was allergic to cow's milk. When I visited them, Grandpa always seemed to be outside in the yard, smoking a cigar or pipe. Apparently, Grandma would not allow him to smoke in the house. He smoked those powerful Italian stogies down to the very end. He'd save the butts in an old coffee can and re-smoke them in his corncob pipe. In winter their kitchen was heated by a large coal fired cast iron stove. A large coal furnace was in the basement.

As was true with most Italian American families, Christmas was always a very special occasion. Grandma was the Matriarch, the "boss" who kept the family together. Her way of celebrating this holiday was to cook a feast that was the grandest of all feasts including fish, pizza, some form of macaroni, sausage and peppers, a variety of vegetables, homemade bread and cookies. Dinner began before midnight mass and continued after mass with the meat dishes.

For most of us those glorious times are a memory, and what a wonderful memory it is.

William LoVerde

∞ Anyone for Spaghetti? ∞

Back in early sixties the stigma of being Italian or Italian American had not really worn off, at least not in our family. In our minds, we had the feeling that Italians were still called "spaghetti benders."

During that period, my dad was in the business of building residential homes and very often his attorney would stop by our house to have dad sign some legal papers. It seemed like every time he came by we were having spaghetti for dinner, thus reinforcing the stereotype.

When we'd see his auto pulling into our driveway, ma would say, "Quick, cover the spaghetti bowl." One of us would immediately jump up, find a lid and cover the spaghetti bowl before the attorney reached the front door. What we did not realize is that the wonderful odor of the spaghetti sauce engulfed the entire house; that special smell that only fresh sauce with spaghetti can provide. After the legal papers had been signed, the attorney always seemed to linger awhile before leaving the house.

In reflecting back, we now believe that he was probably waiting to be invited to dinner and enjoy a plate of spaghetti with us. We regret that we never asked him. Ma is such a great cook, I'm sure his mouth was watering.

Jean Masciangelo

∞ Into the Wild Blue Yonder ∞

My parents are probably responsible for instilling in me the sense of adventure and creativity. At an early age, I had a love of airplanes and was so inspired by Charles Lindberg's, "Spirit of Saint Louis" and his flight across the Atlantic that, at age eight or nine, I decided I wanted to build an airplane. I wanted to build one that I could actually climb into and pretend I was flying.

I scoured the immediate neighborhood for any scraps that I thought I could use for this effort. I collected various sizes of discarded, thin gauge, aluminum pieces from the American Can Company in Fairport, New York along with tomato stakes from my dad's garden, to build the framework of the airplane. The basement of our house became the hangar. By the time I finished the plane, I realized that I would not be able to get it out of the basement. The door from the cellar to the backyard was too narrow. I had to dismantle the wings of the airplane to be able to bring the plane out into the yard. Once all the parts were taken outdoors, I reassembled the airplane on the lawn. All the neighborhood kids came over to my house to sit in the cockpit and enjoy "flying my airplane." I was the most popular kid on the block.

Henry Masciangelo

∞ No Free Lunch ∞

I grew up with my family of five in a sparsely populated area in the town of Henrietta, a suburb of Rochester, New York. In the nineteen twenties and thirties the New York Central railroad passed just a few steps from the side door of our house. Sometimes when the train slowed or came to a complete stop for several minutes, homeless people could be seen jumping off the train looking for food in the neighborhood. During that era, unfortunately, they were referred to as "Hobos." When my mother saw hobos jumping off the train, she would hustle her three children into the house, lock them inside, grab a broom and menacingly wave the broom at the hobos. At the top of her lungs, using her strong broken English, voice she'd yell , "I gotta no fooda to givva to you. You gotta go away!!!" All the drifters would slowly jump back on the train and head west to Buffalo or east to Syracuse. My mother was not a person you would want to mess with.

Mary DiVirgilio Masciangelo

∞ Afterthoughts ∞

As a non-Italian, but an Italophile at heart, I feel privileged to have had the opportunity to contribute, in a very small way, to this collection. The writings chosen for the book, though clearly demonstrating a distinct Italian flavor, show in addition, the universality of the immigrant experience - as shared by my own grandparents. The indelible common theme, to me, is the immigrant's wish for a better life, better education, wider opportunities for their children and the unbelievable efforts and sacrifices willingly made to achieve those ends.

Harriet R. Solit
Editor

∞ Contributors ∞

Bates, Marilyn – is the author of "Mixed Blood,"and is a teacher-consultant with the Western Pennsylvania Writing Project at the University of Pittsburgh. She has contributed to many journals with articles, essays, and reviews. She was appointed as a "Poet in Person" in the Pittsburgh schools and serves on the International Forum's Advisory Board.

Belfiglio, Valentine J. – is a graduate of Albany College of Pharmacy with M.A. and Ph.D. degrees from the University of Oklahoma and served in the United States Army in Vietnam as a Training Officer. He is a professor of Government at the Texas Women's University. In 1982 the President of Italy conferred upon him the title of "Cavaliere dell' Ordine al Merito della Repubblica Italiana" (Knighthood) for his extensive work in promoting Italian culture in the United States.

Belliotti, Raymond A. – has a Ph.D. from the University of Miami and a Law degree from Harvard Law School. He practiced law in New York City for three years, then joined the faculty of the State University of New York at Fredonia, in 1984. He is the Distinguished Teaching Professor of Philosophy at Fredonia, and an author of four books in addition to several articles and reviews.

Belmonte, Peter – is a retired officer of the United States Air Force. He has presented papers at the American Italian Historical Association national conferences and has authored a book, "Italian Americans in World War II." His main research interests involve Calabrian American History and Italian Americans in World War I and II.

Bentivegna, Joseph J. – is a lifelong student of the Italian American experience and a resident of Loreto, PA. In 1973 he founded the Italian Heritage Society which has served as a model for the formation of other organizations. He earned a Ph.D. in Special Education and Rehabilitation and was on the faculty of Saint Francis University. In addition, he has been an instructor of Italian Ethnic Studies and a presenter at national conventions. He is currently in private practice as a Vocational Education Analyst.

Boccacino, Joseph – is a second generation Italian American born on the West Side of Rochester, New York. He is a graduate of Rochester Institute of Technology and was employed for more than forty years as a Tool and Die Designer at the Graflex Corporation.

Calio, Louisa – has an M. Ed. in Urban Studies from Temple University. She is the winner of the 1978 Connecticut Commission of the Arts Award and a founding member and Executive Director of City Spirits Artists, Inc. She has authored several colections of poetry and is editor of senior citizen's and children's writings.

Cappiello, Joseph – is a second generation Italian American and a retired teacher and Guidance Counselor with more than forty-one years in the public school system of New York State. He has an undergraduate degree from the State University of New York at Albany and an M.A. from Harvard University

Cavaioli, Frank J. – is a second generation Italian American with an M.A. and a Ph.D. from Saint John's University. He is a Professor Emeritus from State University of New York at Farmingdale and has published widely including co-editing "The Italian American Experience: An Encyclopedia." He continues to be deeply involved in the American Italian Historical Association and has served several leadership roles within the organization.

Cerasuola, Teresa – was born in Italian Harlem, New York City. She is a third generation Italian American. Since the 1970's, she has been active in various Italian American organizations including the Italian American Historical Association where she has served in various significant capacities. She has written articles on the Arthur Avenue Bronx neighborhood and Neapolitan music, and is currently working on her father's memoirs.

Conforti, Joseph M. – has a Ph.D. in Sociology from Rutgers University. He is a professor and a sociologist teaching at The State University of New York, Old Westbury, Long Island. He is a member of the Executive Council of the American Italian Historical Association. As a sociologist he has published widely in the areas of urban affairs, race and ethnicity, poverty and education.

Correnti, Linda – is an Assistant Principal for Auxiliary Services for High Schools, an alternative program in New York City. Her current research examines the effects of the introduction of the New York State Standards upon staff, students, and administrators of alternative high schools and programs. She is also an adjunct instructor at Fordham University.

Danielle, Vincent A. – received a Ph.D. from Syracuse University. He is a Professor and Chairperson of the Department of Mathematics, College of the National Technical Institute for the Deaf, Rochester Institute of Technology. He is a third generation Italian American and was born and raised in Utica, New York.

Danzi, Angela D. – has a Ph.D. in Sociology from New York University. She is an Associate Professor and Chairperson, Department of Sociology and Anthropology, SUNY Farmingdale. She has written and published widely including contributions to Italian American journals and proceedings. She is a member of the Executive Council of the American Italian Historical Association.

De Angelis, Rose – is an Assistant Professor of English at Marist College and the editor of the book series "Anthropology and Literature." Her interests include Ethnic and American Literature and Gender Studies. Her work on the cultural construction of the Italian female in fiction has appeared in "Forum Italicum and Italian Americana."

DeMatteo, John J. - has both undergraduate and graduate degrees from the City College of New York. He was born in Brooklyn to Gabriele and Carmina DeMatteo. His Italian American parents were born in the United States but moved to and married in Italy. Mr. DeMatteo was employed by the U.S. Navy Department in the Fleet Ballistic Missile Program.

Fagiani, Gil – is a social worker by profession and the Director of Renewal House, a residential treatment program for recovering addicts in Brooklyn. He has published essays and book reviews in several Italian American Journals. He is a poet and short story writer and was selected as a finalist for the Allen Ginsberg Poetry Award.

Fama, Maria – is an author of three books of poetry. Her work appears in numerous publications and has been anthologized She has read her poetry in many cities across the country including on National Public radio and has founded a video production company. For her poem "6:35 A.M" she was named a finalist for the Allen Ginsberg Poetry Award.

Fazio, Vincent – received an undergraduate degree from Syracuse University (Utica Extension) after serving with the U.S. Army in World War II. He is a second generation Italian American and a native of Rochester, New York. He taught high school mathematics for thirty-seven years in the Rochester, New York public school system.

Ferrarelli, Rina – was born in Calabria, Italy and arrived in the United States when she was fifteen years old. She is a graduate of Mount Mercy College and Duquesne University. She has published a book and a chapbook of original poetry "Home is a Foreign Country" and "Dreamsearch," including two books of translated poetry. She received a National Endowment for the Arts grant and the Italo Calvino Prize from the Columbia University Translation Center.

Gala, Edward – is a second generation Italian American born on the West Side of Rochester, New York. He has had an employment career as a businessman and in industry, and currently resides in Florida.

Gala, Frances Romagnolo – is a second generation Italian American and a native of Rochester, New York. She is the wife of Edward Gala, and is a mother and grandmother, and currently resides in Florida.

Gardaphe, Fred L. – directs the Italian American Studies Program at the State University of New York at Stony Brook. He is Associate Editor of Fra Noi, editor of the series in Italian American Studies at SUNY Press and cofounding editor of "Voices in Italian Americana," a literary journal and cultural review. He is an author of several books related to Italians and the Italian American experience and a former president, and a current Executive Council member, of the American Italian Historical Association.

Gennaro, Lou – is Italian American, born in the New York City area. He is a professor and Program Chair in Manufacturing Engineering Technology at Rochester Institute of Technology and is a graduate of the United States Military Academy.

Graf, Virginia Mesolella – is a third generation Italian American born in Rochester, New York and is a retiree from Eastman Kodak Company. She is married and the mother of three boys. Her maternal grandparents were born in Basilicata, Italy and her paternal grandparents in Naples, Italy.

Jackson, Tara – is a fourth generation Italian American. She was born in 1986 in Boston Massachusetts. Tara has excelled in writing and drama starring in many class and school musical productions. She resides with her family in the Rochester, New York area. Her poem "I Am From," written when she was thirteen years old was inspired by a class unit on immigration and the study of Ellis Island. She is very proud of her Sicilian family roots.

Kelly, Jacquelyn Felice – was born in Geneva, New York and currently resides in Fairport, New York. She is a third generation Italian American. She fondly remembers the Italian heritage passed along to her mainly through her maternal and paternal grandparents, her mother and her father. She a professor at Rochester Institute of Technology's National Technical Institute for the Deaf.

Kinch, Carol Ann Vaccarelli – is a third generation Italian American. She was born and raised in Rochester, New York and earned a Bachelor's Degree in English from the State University of New York at Brockport. She, her husband Russ, and their two young daughters live in North Chili, New York. She has wonderful memories of special times with her family and grandparents.

Labozzetta, Marisa – lives in Northampton, MA where she teaches "The Italian-American Experience" at area colleges. She is the author of the novel, "Stay With Me, Lella." Her short stories have appeared in "The American Voice," The Florida Review," and in "VIA."

Labozzetta, Viola Medori – was born in New York City to immigrant parents from Umbria and Calabria. She was employed as a bookkeeper and a secretary for most of her working life. She is the family historian and lives with her husband Michael in Northampton, Massachusetts

LaGumina, Salvatore J. – is a Professor Emeritus from Nassau Community College with M.A. and Ph.D. degrees from Saint John's University. He has been an author or co-editor of more than fourteen books. He is co-editor of "The Italian American Experience: An Encyclopedia," which may be found in the reference section of libraries. His presentations at Italian American national conferences have been numerous and he has served the Italian American Historical Association in a number of significant capacities.

LaPorta, Joseph M. – was born in Sicily. At eighteen months of age he immigrated to the United States with his mother. When he enrolled in elementary school at the age of six, he spoke no English, but he was able to master the language quickly. Lessons received at an early age on the piano and the violin led to a teaching career that spanned more than fifty years. He resides in the Rochester, New York area.

Licata, Don – is a native of the Buffalo, New York area. He is a second generation Italian American whose parents were born in Sicily. He is extremely interested in genealogy and is a charter member of the Western New York chapter of POINT (Pursuing Our Italian Nationality Together).

Lisella, Maria – has been working as a staff writer for twenty-five years reporting on women's politics, health, social justice, and travel. She has been published in "Travel and Leisure," " Journeys," "The New York Daily News," and the "Newark Star Ledger." She has studied in Italy, visits there annually and lectures on the subject of Italian Americans and their travels.

Lotito, Ernest A. – an experienced journalist, whose career has included long term assignments in Italy. He has worked for the "Washington Post" and served as press secretary for former Senator Walter Mondale. He was the Director of Communications for the Corporation for Public Broadcasting and Director of Communications for the Federal Department of Commerce. His "letter" story first appeared in I-AM Magazine in 1978 and has also been published in the National Italian American Foundation Newsletter.

LoVerde, William – is a product of the West Side of Rochester, New York. He is a graduate of Thomas Jefferson High School, served as a medic during the Vietnam conflict, and has been an employee of the United States Postal Service for more than twenty-five years.

Lyon, Diane Francesconi – is an Adjunct Professor of History at Montgomery College in Rockville, MD. She is a graduate of The College of Notre Dame of Maryland and Marquette University. She has been an Assistant Editor for the Charles Carroll of Carrollton and John Carroll Papers.

Mancusi, Reverend Michael – is a Barnibite priest who was born in Brooklyn, New York, studied at the Vatican in Rome, Italy and was ordained in 1979. He has an M.Ed. from Canisius College in Buffalo, New York and taught in a catholic school for twelve years before being assigned as pastor of Saint James Parish in Oakville, Ontario, Canada.

Mannino, Mary Ann – has a Ph.D. in British and American Literature from Temple University. She is a university Instructor, an author of books and critical articles, a poet and a fiction writer.

Marino, Charles H. – is a second generation Italian American. He was born of Sicilian parents on Rochester, New York's West Side. He has an undergraduate degree from the University of Rochester and a medical degree from the University of Buffalo. He has had professional experience in the field of OB-GYN for more than forty-seven years.

Marino, Richard – whose grandparents were born in Calabria, Italy, was born in the Bronx and attended school in New York City. He has an undergraduate degree from Lehman College and is a librarian at the main San Francisco, California Library.

Marino, Teresa – is a second generation Italian American who was born in Donora, Pennsylvania. At nine months of age she moved with her family to the East Side of Rochester, New York. She is an interior decorator and a mother with ten children and twenty grandchildren.

Maruggi, Carolyn Baumgartner. – is married to a second generation Italian American. She has a bachelor's degree in History from Jacksonville University, Florida. A prize-winning designer and producer of quilts, she is a fabric artist, who is active in local quilt guilds. She is a retired certified appraiser of quilts.

Maruggi, Edward Albert – is a second generation Italian American with undergraduate and graduate degrees from SUNY Oswego and a Ph.D. from the University of Minnesota. He is a Professor Emeritus from Rochester Institute of Technology, a textbook author, and was formerly a mechanical engineer in Industry. He is on the Executive Council of the American Italian Historical Association and a member of the Sons of Italy, Lombardi Chapter.

Maruggi, Edward P. – is a third generation Italian American. He has undergraduate and graduate degrees from Rochester Institute of Technology. His professional career includes that of a college professor and software specialist at Rochester Institute of Technology. He is currently employed as a computer analyst.

Masciangelo, Henry - is a second generation Italian American and lives in Fairport, New York. He served in the Pacific Theater with the U. S. Corps of Engineers during World War II. He is a former home builder in Fairport and currently operates a sports complex facility which he founded in 1987.

Masciangelo, Jean - is a third generation Italian American who was born and still lives in Fairport, New York. She is a graduate of Arizona State University and is employed in her family's sports complex facility.

Masciangelo, Mary DiVirgilio - is a second generation Italian American and graduated from James Monroe High School in Rochester, New York. She lives in Fairport, New York with her husband, Henry. She enjoys sewing, gardening, and working in the family business.

Mautner, Raeleen D'Agostino – has a Ph.D. and is founder of "Italy-U.S. Connection: Research and Training." With the collaboration of national and international colleagues, IUC offers survey research and cross-cultural training seminars to U.S. and Italian companies.

Mileo, Joseph – was born and raised by Sicilian immigrant parents on the East Side of Rochester, New York. He is a graduate of Niagara University and a World War II Army veteran of the China, India, Burma Theater. He had an extensive career in the building supplies business, construction, land development, and real estate.

Morante, Nick – is a second generation Italian American born on the West Side of Rochester, New York. He is a graduate of Madison High School, and a U.S. Navy veteran of World War II. His employment career was in the chemical industry. He resides with is wife in Prattsburgh, New York and in Florida.

Morreale, Frank – is an artist whose work reflects the Italian renaissance in its attention to surface richness and its fusion of eastern and western influences. He was born in Chicago and attended the University of Chicago as well as The School of the Art Institute of Chicago. His work has been displayed in art galleries and shows in New York, Chicago, Paris, and Tokyo.

Natale, Vincent – is a Professor Emeritus of Psychology from Monroe Community College and former supervisor of student teachers at the State University of New York at Brockport. He is a second generation Italian American, born on the West Side of Rochester, New York. He served in the United States Merchant Marine.

Novara, Elenor Migliazzo – is a second generation Italian American who was born in Niagara, Falls, New York and still resides there. Her grandparents emigrated from Sicily in 1909. She is a member of the Buffalo and Western New York Genealogy Society.

Oliviero, Toni H. – is a second generation Italian American and is a member of the English and Humanities Department and Dean of the College of Liberal Arts and Sciences at Pratt Institute in New York City.

Ortolani, Vincent – was born and raised in an Italian American neighborhood in Rochester, New York. His father Vincent emigrated around 1900 from Valledolmo, Sicily, at the age of six. His mother Epifania Micciche Ortolani arrived in the U.S. in 1920. He is a private school and college graduate and is currently a professor at the National

Technical Institute for the Deaf at Rochester Institute of Technology.

Parlato, Jr. Sal – is a retired teacher of English as a Second Language. He is a sometime poet and has been published in numerous journals and reviews. He has written and published a book on deafness. In addition, he worked in the field of captioning for deaf students in Washington, District of Columbia.

Pellegrino, Marian - is a second generation Italian American who was born in Revere, MA and moved to the Rochester, New York area as a child. She attended Saint Anthony's catholic grammar school and graduated from Benjamin Franklin High School. Her major employment was as an executive secretary at Rochester General Hospital.

Poletti, David - is a second generation Italian American who was born and still resides in Fairport, New York. He is a graduate of Fairport High School and is associated with the Steamfitters union. He is proud to be an Italian American.

Re, Vittorio – was born in Australia to a family of Lombard descent. He has a bachelor's degree in History and is a Knight in the Order of Merit in the Italian Republic. He is the founder of the Italian Cultural Center in Michigan and a contributor to its monthly newspaper. His current interest is in the preservation of Italian records in Michigan.

Sartori, Gloria A. – is a third generation Italian American. Her ancestors are from northern and central Italy. She was born and educated in Buffalo. New York and was employed for most of her working life as a legal secretary for a large law firm.

Sciolino, Anthony - is a second generation Italian American who was born in Rochester, New York. He is a Family Court Judge, former Assistant District Attorney, and has a law degree from Cornell University Law School. He also has an M.A. in Theology from Saint Bernard's Institute and is a Deacon at the Church of the Transfiguration in Pittsford, New York.

Smith, Roslyn Piazza - is a second generation Italian American who was born in Rochester, New York and currently resides in Brockport, New York. She loves to quilt and is a member of one of the oldest quilt clubs in the United States.

Solit, Harriet R. - resides in Cambridge, Massachusetts, attended the School of the Museum of Fine Arts in Boston, Syracuse University, and Boston University and has been a working artist almost all her life. An admirer of the Italian language and culture, and frequent traveler to Italy, she is planning to exhibit her Italian water colors in Pinerolo (TO) and Calabria in May 2004.

Spinelli, Rose - is an independent writer and and producer. After returning to Sant 'Ambrogio, Sicily, her ancestral roots, she documented and produced a film, "Baking Bread" which is currrently in post production.

Stokes, Susan Maruggi – is a third generation Italian American born on the West Side of Rochester, New York. She is a graduate of Fairport High School and attended Canton Institute of Technology, Canton, New York. Her paternal grandparents were born in Basilicata, Italy and her maternal grandparents in Frosinone, Italy.

Taylor, Francesca – was born and resides in the Los Angeles area. Her maternal grandparents were from Calabria, in southern Italy. She is currently an Assistant Professor of Family Medicine at the University of Southern California and Director of Maternity Services for one of the Department's affiliated residency training programs in downtown Los Angeles.

Toscano, Antonio - is a first generation Italian American. He is the designer of the cover for this book. He has an undergraduate degree from the Museum Art School in Portland, Oregon and a graduate degree from Rochester Institute of Technology where he is employed as a professor. He resides in Rochester, New York.

Treitel, Renata - was born in Lausanne, Switzerland and was educated in Italy, the United States, and Argentina She is currently employed as a teacher, poet and translator. and resides in Tulsa, Oklahoma.

∞ Photo Credits ∞

Pen and Ink Sketch - Tuscan Hillltop town of Monteriggione by Harriet R. Solit, page viii.

Lucia Means Light - photo of grandma Lucia Antonini and grandpa Marco contributed by grandaughter Louisa Calio, page 15.

The General - photo of Ma Mileo contributed by son Joseph Mileo, page 46.

The Italian Wedding - photo and contribution of Roslyn Piazza Smith on her wedding day, page 68.

Uncle Larry's Funeral - photo of Larry Vaccarelli contributed by the Vacarelli family, page 89.

Grandma Yogi - photo of grandma Teresa Maruggi contributed by grandson Edward P. Maruggi, page 126.

The Spizzirri Family Odessy: From Italy to America - photo of great grandparents Spizzirri and grandson Giacomo contributed by great grandson Peter Belmonte, page147.

Mama the Gourmet Cook - photo of Ma Sciolino contributed by son Anthony Sciolino, page 165.

Grandma's Ritual - Photo of grandma Felice and grandchildren contributed by grandaughter Jacqueline Felice Kelly, page 190.

Remembering Pa - photo of Pa and Ma Natale contributed by son Vincent Natale, page 200.

Reflections - photo of the Fazio family. Eight sons in military service in World War II and the Korean war. Contribution of Vincent Fazio, page 224.

Book Order Form

Italian Heart, American Soul
An Anthology

Ordered by: _____

_____

_____

_____

Send to: (if different from above)

_____

_____

_____

_____

Quantity ordered: _____ @ $14.95 = _____

New York State residents add 8%
sales tax to the above amount. _____

Add $2.50 shipping for one book,
$1.00 for each additional book. _____

Payment by: Check ____ Money Order _____

Mail this form and Payment to:

WINSTON PUBLISHING
52 TOBEY COURT
PITTSFORD, NEW YORK 14534-1857
Phone: 585-385-1905 Fax: 585-385-7953
www.winstonpublishing.us
email: winston@winstonpublishing.us